COMMERCIAL LEASES

COMMERCIAL LEASES

Second Edition

David Cockburn
Former Senior Partner, Archibald Campbell & Harley

Robin Mitchell
Partner, Archibald Campbell & Harley

Bloomsbury Professional

Bloomsbury Professional Limited, Maxwelton House, 41–43 Boltro Road, Haywards Heath, West Sussex, RH16 1BJ

© Bloomsbury Professional Limited 2011

Bloomsbury Professional, an imprint of Bloomsbury Publishing Plc

A CIP Catalogue record for this book is available from the British Library.

ISBN: 978 184766 317 7

Typeset by Phoenix Photosetting, Chatham, Kent
Printed and bound by CPI Group (UK) Ltd, Croydon, CR0 4YY

Preface

The objective of this edition remains that of providing practical advice in relation to the negotiation of the documentation required for occupational leases of commercial property. The last few years have seen the emergence of a code for business leases in England and codes of practice for service charges there and in Scotland, such that a welcome degree of standardisation is emerging, albeit not yet leading to any obvious reduction in the variety of lease styles in common use. We focus on the issues that arise in the adjustment and negotiation of such leases, whatever the style, and examine the reasons for the commercial positions adopted by advisers to the parties.

There have been a number of important changes since the last edition in 2002, some dictated by market influences. In general, the demands of clients for swift contracts in an increasingly mature market has compelled the production of more balanced documentation and more realistic negotiations. The downturn in the property market has shortened lease lengths and turned the court spotlight on break clauses. 'Green leases' which have been slow to develop due to the reluctance of landlords to advance to a small pool of tenants documentation with potentially adverse cost implications are now gaining ground due to the impetus of environmental legislation, certainly in the office market. Changes in the Competition Act affect matters such as exclusivity clauses. We have also witnessed the need to grapple with the niceties of SDLT in replacing the more benign stamp duty regime.

We have tried to cover these and other changes, while retaining the need to reflect a sense of priority that needs to be at the heart of any negotiations intended to produce a commercially sound outcome. In that respect, although modern rent review clauses now contain many standard assumptions and disregards, they remain potential sources of dispute and their evolution is treated at some length.

Thanks for their patience is due both to our publishers and to our secretary, Susan Husband.

David Cockburn
Robin Mitchell
August 2011

Contents

Contents

Table of statutory materials and guidance

Table of statutory materials and guidance

Table of cases

Table of cases

Chapter 1

General Introduction

1.1 More than half a century has passed since we began to import from England the form of lease of commercial property which made the tenant responsible, directly or indirectly, for the whole costs of repairing (and if necessary rebuilding) the subjects of lease and of insuring them. Such leases, initially in new developments likely to be financed by major institutions, endured for 25 years and contained detailed provisions for upward only rent reviews; they became known as 'institutional leases'. They have been the subject of much criticism over the years on grounds of their length and apparent complexity, their perceived bias in favour of powerful landlords and the inordinate time taken to adjust the detailed terms. During the last decade of the twentieth century, the market began to demand change, given added emphasis by alterations to accountancy practice disclosing leases on balance sheets. Lease lengths began to decrease and tenant break options became more common, a trend that accelerated markedly in the challenging economic conditions later in the next decade. Attempts at standardisation of lease styles have largely failed but the property industry has, however belatedly, come to understand that the wider interests of landlord and tenant are best served by the early adjustment of leasehold documentation that fairly balances their respective interests. To that end, there is now a lease code for England and Wales[1] which is having some general influence in Scotland and which emphasises the need for clarity in both negotiations and in final documentation and whose detailed recommendations are intended to promote fairness. That said, the upward only rent review clause (the object of much criticism) continues in leases of more than five years despite exhortations that landlords should provide alternatives. Parties and their advisers now also have the benefit of a Scottish edition of a code of practice applying to service charges published in 2007 (soon to be replaced by a UK wide version) and to which detailed reference appears in Chapter 6.

---

1   The Code for Leasing Business Premises in England and Wales 2007.

1

1.2 Against that background, it may be hoped that the adjustment of leases will become increasingly less disputative with solicitors for landlords submitting documents that both reflect the terms agreed and recognise the legitimate concerns of tenants. In turn, those representing tenants should acknowledge the submission of balanced documentation and resist the temptations of unnecessary revisal. In pursuit of these objectives lawyers must have regard to clients' expectations of early deals at reasonable fee rates. Indeed the ready adjustment of leases by experienced and pragmatic solicitors has always existed; it may be that the agreement is the document that demands time as it needs to reflect the terms negotiated for the property concerned, including the access and entry dates, rent review dates, rent free period, links to other lettings and such like all of which can have immediate financial impact upon the parties on an unexpected outcome.

1.3 However, despite the commercial pressures for sensible change, one needs to recognise that leasehold documentation will, particularly in multi-occupancy developments, remain somewhat complex and continue to demand care, as can be seen from the documentation list in paragraph 1.4. New commercial imperatives, for example the attraction to tenants of break options, have spawned court challenges, historic rent review clauses still need interpretation and implementation, so-called virtual assignments have appeared and there is the need for leases to reflect modern environmental concerns. The statutory background to 'green leases' that try specifically to address the environmental impacts of a building, will be considered generally in Chapter 9. The provisions that are emerging as suitable for such leases are discussed at or near to the end of each chapter to which they are relevant but at this early stage of development, their precise terms and their positioning in leases is not settled. In general they reflect a growing, but as yet in Scotland, a cautious response to a system that offers obvious benefits to landlords and tenants but which is not without practical difficulty.

1.4 The most daunting feature of the modern occupational commercial lease is the length of the required documentation of which the lease itself is only one component. Where the property to be leased is part of a sophisticated development which at the point of production of the drafts may not be in the ownership of the developer or the subject of a planning permission, let alone actually built, the 'package' of drafts may contain many of the following:

(i)   offer (or agreement) to lease;

(ii)   specification and drawings of developer's proposed works;

(iii)   collateral warranties with letters of appointment (and building contracts);

(iv)   fitting-out licence;

(v)   tenant's guide for fitting out;

(vi)   lease;

(vii)   back letter(s);

(viii) latent defect specimen policy;

(ix)   step-in agreement;

(x)   rent deposit guarantee;

(xi)   guarantee.

1.5 Many of the documents in this package, particularly the lease, will be of considerable length and together they represent a challenge for the solicitors acting for both landlord and tenant despite the welcome trend mentioned in paragraph 1.2. Unfortunately, the extent of the task for the tenant is sometimes made unnecessarily demanding by the landlord's solicitor succumbing to the temptation of seeking the protection of a long style of lease with which he or she and/or the client is familiar and paying too little attention to the precise type of lease required to fulfil the underlying commercial terms. Caution is understandable where the 'landlord' is a developer intent on selling the completed development as soon as convenient. The advisers to such a landlord must ensure that the package of documents, particularly the lease which will survive for a substantial period, does not contain any provisions which might cause a future purchaser to reject the deal. But the production of styles, not drafts, can sometimes produce draconian terms for leases of unsophisticated built property at low rental, and of limited duration, and in all cases adds to the workload of the tenant's solicitor. In an effort to obtain an early bargain on favourable terms the landlord's solicitor may also issue the offer as a principal containing a time limit, a procedure which sits uneasily with the need of the parties to achieve agreement on every word in the package. Some tenants' solicitors, instead of treating the offer properly as a draft, are tempted either to issue a qualified acceptance referring to a revised draft lease (which would lead to a highly convoluted bargain) or accept unconditionally, in the erroneous expectation that they can adjust the draft lease later, only then to be faced with the landlord's solicitor pointing to a concluded contract.

1.6 The tenant's solicitor also faces temptations. He or she may assume, sometimes incorrectly, that such a lengthy professionally produced series of documents must be technically sound and, possibly fortified by comments from the landlord's solicitor to this effect, may reach the conclusion that these 'standard' documents are not capable of being changed, particularly if the client is not a powerful player in the marketplace. The tenant's solicitor may also be concerned at the profitability of the transaction because of the time required to consider these documents carefully, let alone examine a sophisticated title (and relative permissions) to a much larger development of which the proposed subjects of lease form a very limited part.

1.7 The consequences of concluding contracts without qualification or limiting these to the insertion of 'reasonable' throughout the documentation at appropriate intervals can be serious. Common sense dictates that major tenants are able to demand more significant adjustments to leasehold documentation than are those in a commercially weaker position but working for the latter rarely means that no material changes can be made and never does it require that no attempt should be made. All clients, be they landlord or tenant, should be made aware of the general extent of their rights and obligations under any potential contract and although the reporting techniques which solicitors need to use will vary depending upon the knowledge and experience of the client, that obligation upon the solicitor remains undiluted.

1.8 In summary, solicitors for landlords should produce a package of properly drawn drafts reflecting the terms agreed between the parties or their advisers. Solicitors acting for tenants should consult the client and its surveyors and other advisers on the accuracy and applicability of the various specifications, drawings, tenant's guide for fitting out etc, take copies of the legal drafts and revise these to reflect the agreed terms and his/her experience.

1.9 Leases (including agreements) are documents which throughout their life will be much examined for such as rent review or alienation and where important commercial interests can turn on their interpretation. Clear, concise and, if possible, non repetitive drafting is to be preferred. In particular, accurate and consistent use of defined terms, preferably at the start of the lease, reduces its length and assists ready understanding, particularly by management surveyors.

1.10 It is unsurprising that, given that such leases are an import from England, attention is paid to developments there, particularly in areas such as rent review where there has been much activity. Distinct differences between the two systems remain and the Scottish courts have asserted unequivocally that they do not intend to abandon any principles of our system to satisfy an argument for a unified approach based on some notion of public policy. Readers will accordingly understand that the English cases to which reference is made in the text require to be treated with some degree of caution. Fears expressed in the past that in Scotland our courts may lack a sufficiently detailed knowledge of the custom and practice of modern property law and that this will lead to decisions that lack commercial reality may with the passage of time have been allayed.

Chapter 2

Offers or Agreements for Lease

GENERAL

2.1 Whether the landlord's solicitor, in drawing the documentation, prepares the draft of an offer to lease or an agreement to lease is largely a matter of personal choice, although many practitioners would agree that the style of an agreement is better suited to the more sophisticated form of development, particularly if there are intended to be more than two contracting parties. Neither, when using an agreement, must one forgo the advantage of using missives to provide a speedy contract. Brief missives can easily be concluded between the parties' solicitors, binding on both parties and requiring their respective clients to execute an agreement in terms of the draft annexed within a particular timescale, or alternatively simply acknowledging that the terms of the agreement are binding without the actual deed being executed subsequently. For the sake of convenience, this chapter proceeds on the basis that the parties enter into an agreement for lease. Sometimes it is suggested in particular transactions that the solicitors for the parties need agree only the terms of the lease and have their clients execute it, rendering any missives or agreement for lease unnecessary. This most frequently occurs when dealing with secondary or tertiary property, often with a lease of relatively short duration. However, the concept is fundamentally flawed. Not only does this lead to potential delay before the parties are legally committed (with a temptation to allow the tenant prior entry) but it fails particularly from the tenant's angle to trigger items such as a good title, evidence of statutory notices etc. At the other end of the spectrum, where parties are entering into an agreement for lease in advance of any development taking place or even the necessary statutory consents being available, the agreement becomes very complicated. Indeed, experienced practitioners usually find it more difficult to adjust the agreement than the lease. Leases often follow a fairly common pattern but each agreement is site-specific, significantly dependent upon terms negotiated by the respective clients' surveyors which are not always totally free from doubt and frequently (mostly for the tenant) require considerable additional drafting, not merely the adjustment and/or excision of existing clauses.

THE PARTIES

2.2 Often the parties to the agreement will be identical to those who will execute the lease, particularly when the subjects of lease are in existence and the period between the execution of the agreement and the lease is short (para 2.31). However, a developer entering into agreements with potential tenants of a development not yet started may intend to sell its investment as soon as it is income-producing (and to contract to do so even earlier). Because the agreement is a personal contract between or among the parties, a number of points are worthy of mention:

(i)   It is usual for the developer to satisfy itself on the 'covenant' of the tenant prior to instructing its solicitor, although the solicitor should be clear on that subject before commitment, certainly if his/her client is inexperienced.

(ii)   A tenant can become committed for a period of years (and thereby be excluded from considering alternative locations) while awaiting the construction of the development, so that some consideration should be given by the tenant as to the ability of the developer to undertake substantial development obligations within an acceptable timescale, particularly when the developer company may be a single-purpose vehicle incorporated specifically for the relevant development and the advent of access dates increases the tenant's expenditure prior to acquiring a real right (para 2.13). The extent of the investigation and the need for any guarantees from third parties will depend on the circumstances.

(iii)   The solicitor for the developer should recognise that any purchaser of the let investment will not want to be obliged (as opposed to having the option) to complete any development obligations unfulfilled by the developer.

(iv)   It is common for agreements to reinforce the doctrine of *delectus personae* by spelling out that they are personal to the tenant. Although major tenants sometimes extract an agreement that they may substitute another comparable tenant within the same group, the landlord should usually resist, certainly if any substitute would result in a change of trading style. The developer may reasonably insist on the right to assign to any party demonstrably able to fulfil its side of the bargain with a 'step-in' agreement (of which an adjusted draft should be annexed) being used if the possible purchaser (or a heritable creditor) is capable of identification. Tenants usually have no objection in principle to giving a party such as a bank the opportunity to step into the developer's shoes, as the exercise probably enhances the likelihood of the development being completed; the tenant should ensure that the bank exercises the right quickly and only on the basis of assuming all of the developer's obligations under the existing agreement. Agreements will often state that in the event of breach by the developer, the tenant is not entitled to rescind the contract if step-in rights are taken up within a certain period of time. A tenant should generally have no difficulty with this, but should ensure that the right to determine the contract in the event of failure by the developer to meet a long stop date is not lost through such a provision.

LANDLORD'S TITLE

2.3 To take the lease outwith the realms of a personal contract so that a real right is conferred upon the tenant, the landlord's title must be good. The agreement should contain an obligation upon the landlord to exhibit a valid marketable title to the subjects of lease (or, where applicable, to the development of which they form a part) in the same way as in an offer to purchase commercial property, including provisions for clear searches in the property, personal and charges registers. An appropriate letter of obligation to be granted by the landlord's solicitors should be adjusted. A few points arise from this relatively common concept:

(i)   Many modern agreements for new developments provide for tenants to obtain access many weeks prior to a date of entry triggered by a certificate of practical completion (para 2.13). Because the tenant may spend considerable sums on fitting out prior to entry under the lease, it is sensible to provide that the title obligations of the landlord should be implemented prior to the access date and, by updating, at the entry date.

(ii) It is almost inevitable that in the annexed draft lease the obligations of the tenant will include that of complying with all the burdens and restrictions in the title; and in the event that the title has not been exhibited to the tenant prior to the agreement being concluded, the agreement should, as with a purchase, either require that the title contains no burdens materially adverse to the interest of the tenant, or (as is more likely) enable the tenant to rescind the agreement if within any particular timescale it is not satisfied on the subject.

(iii) If the searches reveal that there is a heritable creditor, the landlord should be required to exhibit the standard security and the creditor's consent in appropriate terms[1]. Likewise, a letter of non-crystallisation will be required from the holder of any floating charge, containing, inter alia, consent by such holder to the grant of the lease

(iv) The landlord may not be the heritable proprietor. An examination of title may reveal that it is a principal tenant or even a more subordinate tenant in a convoluted leasehold chain. If so, the tenant's solicitor must examine not only the title of the party so vest but also every element of that chain, not only for pure 'title' matters but also to consider the question of any consents to the occupational lease which may need to be obtained. The tenant's solicitor must also in these circumstances consider the next point.

(v) England has statutory protections available but, in Scotland, when a lease falls, all subordinate leases automatically fall. In practice, a landlord faced with the demise of a principal tenant may wish to enter into leases with the various occupational sub-tenants on existing terms to preserve its income stream but there is no guarantee, particularly in a rising rental market. If the landlord is itself a tenant, the tenant should ask for an undertaking by the head landlord, agreeing to enter into a new lease on identical terms should the superior lease fall, and to be liable in damages on a failure to take a purchaser of the head landlord's interest similarly bound. The head landlord may prefer in these circumstances to trigger a new lease rather than simply confer an option upon the tenant. By this method (assuming that all leases in the development are so structured) the landlord will retain a let investment rather than allow certain tenants to escape from a property which may not suit their needs. Further, the situation becomes complicated when there is a leasehold chain with a variety of parties involved.

(vi) There is a practical difficulty associated with title examination. If the tenant is taking a lease of a very minor unit in, say, a major shopping centre whose title was acquired by complex site assembly, possibly involving the creation of a variety of leasehold interests, the tenant's solicitor may, with justification, consider that he or she cannot realistically undertake a full title examination. For obvious commercial reasons, this is less of a difficulty for those solicitors who act for a number of the tenants in the development. If any tenant's solicitor feels unable to conduct a proper examination of title, he/she should explain clearly in writing to the client the limitations in the work able to be undertaken for the agreed fee, leaving the client to consider the financial implications of a full examination and instruct accordingly. In recent years, for the sake of expediency, the solicitors acting for the landlords of some major developments have issued certificates of title at settlement, thus avoiding the need for any title examination by the tenant's solicitors. This however remains rare.

---

1   *Trade Development Bank v Warriner & Mason (Scotland) Ltd* 1980 SC 74, 1980 SLT 223.

SUBJECTS OF LEASE

2.4 As is discussed in Chapter 3, the extent of the property being leased, with any pertinents to be enjoyed and reservations and exceptions to apply, should all appear in detail in the lease itself, as should the extent of the development of which the subjects of lease form part. However, if the agreement deals with a property not yet built, then not only must the agreement contain (para 2.6) detailed obligations upon the landlord as to construction but it should properly take account of potential variations in size. The landlord should not accept an obligation to build a unit of specific dimensions, although certain tenants of retail properties require a minimum width of unit so as to accommodate their standard size sales browsers with prescribed distances between them. Generally, however, the parties will agree the approximate size and the rent per square feet of gross internal area to be applied. Upper and lower tolerance figures for each level, if applicable (and requiring greater flexibility in a sophisticated multi-storey development than in, say, an industrial estate), should be agreed so as to allow to the tenant an option of terminating the agreement in the unlikely event of the landlord failing to meet the parameters. The tenant may also try to fix a ceiling on the rent (and possibly also after review) at the upper tolerance figure should the tenant wish to proceed and not terminate. The landlord may adopt a different posture! Usually, on failure by the parties to agree the gross internal area, the matter would be determined by an expert with reference to the prevailing Code of Measuring Practice of the Royal Institution of Chartered Surveyors.

SUSPENSIVE CONDITIONS

2.5 In developments such as major shopping centres it is common for the developer's solicitor to be invited to submit at an early stage in the process the leasehold package in draft form to solicitors acting for the more important proposed tenants. The developer may not then have missives to acquire all of the required land, any existing contracts may be heavily conditional, and a raft of consents (including planning permission) may be necessary. The developer's solicitor will try to ensure that the agreement contains suspensive conditions on all of these matters and also possibly relative to the letting of a minimum proportion of the development, and to settling the various purchases and entering into letters of appointment with the professional team members and the building contract with a suitable contractor. The developer's solicitor may provide that these clauses operate for the benefit of the developer alone so that they can be waived[1] in whole or in part and that each component should be resolved to the absolute satisfaction of the developer in its sole discretion. Provisions in these terms arguably equate to an option in favour of the developer; nevertheless, sensible tenants recognise that the developer needs protection. Many of the tenant's fears can be allayed by:

(i)   replacing the clause relative to settling the various purchases with one requiring them only to have concluded contracts for such purchases. Conditionality on actually settling purchases is derived from the English system, any risk must be very small and if this principle were applied throughout commercial contracts much less certainty would prevail;

(ii)   eliminating the clause dealing with the building contract and letters of appointment which is a mask to disguise concerns about escalating building costs. The timescale is in the hands of the developer and the end users can reasonably argue that the developer's return should reflect some risk;

(iii)   considering closely the extent to which other pre-lets and their timing feature. Although superficially appealing, eliminating this clause or reducing the proportion may not be to the tenant's advantage as a poorly let development would be commercially to the disadvantage of the tenant who might wish to ensure that such a suspensive clause with right to resile was inserted for its benefit too;

(iv)   producing a series of time constraints by which each such suspensive condition could realistically be removed with a measure of safety. However, tenants should guard against their agreements falling and being replaced by other agreements with rival tenants at enhanced rents;

(v)   allowing input from the tenant as to the acceptability of the grant of planning permission. Tenants need to guard against the permission or an associated agreement under Section 75 of the Town and Country Planning (Scotland) Act 1997, as amended by the Planning etc (Scotland) Act 2006 restricting use, imposing limitations on servicing or trading hours, reducing car parking spaces or changing access arrangements to the operational disadvantage of the tenant. Some tenants have standard lists of onerous conditions.

If the result of the discussions on the clause dealing with suspensive conditions is to leave to the developer the right to escape, particularly in respect of its non-acquisition of the required properties, some tenants will wish to insist upon repayment of abortive expenses, certainly legal costs, if the developer landlord exercises its option.

---

1   *Manheath Ltd v H J Banks & Co Ltd* 1996 SLT 1006, 1996 SCLR 100 (1 DIV).

DEVELOPER'S/LANDLORD'S OBLIGATIONS OF CONSTRUCTION OR REPAIR

2.6 It may be that, in respect of a property already built, the landlord agrees to carry out certain works of alterations or repair, in which event questions arise about a specification to identify the works, quality control, necessary consents and a procedure for agreeing that the obligations of the landlord have been properly fulfilled, thereby triggering entry. But it is in the context of an agreement for a property (or part) not yet constructed that all of these (and other) issues are raised in sharp focus.

2.7 Sometimes the initial draft agreement is drawn by the landlord's solicitor either to eliminate such obligations (by focusing drafting on obligations of the tenant to take the property on an access date or practical completion date) or so dilute them as to offer the tenant too little protection. In some major developments the obligations upon the tenant to fit out the unit (by the application of a draft licence attached to the agreement) are more lengthy and onerous than those applied to the developer to build the whole development; it is submitted that no well-advised developer should or need proceed in this way.

2.8 The tenant's solicitor must ensure that his/her client confirms in writing its satisfaction with the specification and drawings but these are likely to relate to the property being leased, not to the whole development, whether a shopping centre, business park or office block. But if 'the Works' (or similar definition) relates solely to such a specification and drawings, the tenant is not contractually entitled to anything more. This may be less important where in office blocks or shopping centres it may not be practical to build part only and the tenant may take comfort that notwithstanding its solicitor's failure to extend 'the Works' beyond the subjects of lease, the whole development will be finished. But in, say, a retail park the developer may intend to build out the whole development only as and when market forces dictate and, if asked by the tenant's solicitor, may resist change. However, to draw the agreement (as some do) in such a way as to avoid all obligations beyond the unit itself is unrealistic. The tenant needs to ensure that, before its date of entry is triggered, the unit is complete as are sufficient of the common parts, for example car park areas, access roads and the like, to enable it to trade, and it would be unwise to rely solely on planning conditions guaranteeing that result. Even then, trading from a solus unit is not generally what the tenant envisaged and it may require completion of a guaranteed proportion of the development and/ or discounts on rent until such time as a certain number of units in the development are open and trading. The occupation of the subjects of lease where construction continues on nearby properties raises some practical considerations and it may be necessary to annex a construction method statement designed from the tenant's angle to ensure the continuation of its facilities and the absence of material disruption.

2.9 The tenant will want the developer to carry out the works (however defined) free of cost to the tenant, in a good and workmanlike manner, using good quality and appropriate materials and in accordance with all relevant consents, all relevant legislation and the Construction (Design and Management) Regulations 1994. In particular, no prohibited (formerly called deleterious) materials, the list whereof varies according to the prevailing knowledge and the particular requirements of individual clients, should be used. Developers should try to avoid themselves granting any such obligation and instead point to the availability of collateral warranties (paras 2.23–2.30).

2.10 The initial draft agreement as submitted is unlikely to require the developer to complete construction work within any particular timescale, thereby avoiding a tenant's escape route unwelcome to both the developer and the source of any interim finance. However, the tenant needs some certainty. It is usually accepted that the developer should use reasonable endeavours or all reasonable endeavours, as opposed to 'best endeavours' (the judgement in *Mactaggart & Mickel Homes Ltd v Hunter*[1] having confirmed the hierarchy of such expressions) to ensure that a certificate of practical completion of the works is issued by a sensible target date and that failure by the developer to finish by a further 'long stop' date results in termination of the agreement or (preferably from the tenant's angle) a tenant's option to terminate. If the latter, the developer must ensure that the notice of termination is served within a restricted timescale of the end date and bites only if it pre-dates the completion of the works. In fixing the long stop date both parties should err on the side of caution. Badly timed insured risk damage or major labour or contractual disputes could result in the loss to the developer of an anchor tenant and the collapse of the development. Conversely, premature termination of the tenant's bargain may suit the developer in a rising rental market. The objective of these provisions is not to penalise the developer but to avoid either party being locked into a development about which there are real concerns as to its completion.

---

1   [2010] CSOH 130.

2.11 In the gestation period between the execution of the agreement and the construction of the development, construction practices or the availability of materials or the tenant's standard requirements for fitting-out purposes may have varied. The developer should therefore have the right to vary the works, particularly external to the subjects being leased, and usually provisos about reasonableness and maintenance of quality standards are capable of adjustment. A developer should have some flexibility on the layout of the development and, subject to planning constraints, should be able to change unit sizes (but not the subjects of lease) as the letting programme progresses. That said, a tenant may require that certain elements, for example car parking numbers and location and access to the subjects of lease, remain constant. This may be particularly important in a shopping mall where changing access routes may dramatically alter footfall. Of course, after the lease is granted, it will regulate such reservations (para 3.16). It is reasonable for the tenant to require the developer to carry out the developer's works subject to modifications or additions required by the tenant but the developer has to ensure that proper detail is given, they do not involve to an unreasonable extent the undoing of work already in course, they do not cause substantial delay or inconvenience and they do not detrimentally affect the works. If these criteria are met and in particular the tenant pays directly and indirectly incurred costs, the developer should have no difficulty. Often, the parties will agree that any variation required by the tenant is to be fully costed before being agreed, with the tenant being liable for the costs of such calculation as well as the costs of the variation, if agreed. The tenant will wish to ensure that its costs are limited to the figure estimated. Specific regard to these items should be paid when considering the rent review clause as to whether or to what extent such works should be rentalised.

2.12 The agreement should afford to the tenant and its authorised representatives the right to gain access on appropriate notice to the subjects in the course of construction, to attend meetings as an observer, to monitor the progress of the developer's works and to make representations thereanent. Such clauses have clear impact in respect of access and practical completion.

ACCESS DATE/PRACTICAL COMPLETION/ENTRY/ RENT-FREE PERIODS

2.13 In former times, agreements proceeded on the basis that the tenant took physical occupation on the issue of a certificate of practical completion of the subjects of lease and of any other parts of the development which the developer was obliged to construct and that in terms of the building contract. Although this procedure was (and remains so) a matter upon which there was some potential for dispute, it had the advantage of clarity. When the certificate was properly issued the date of entry became fixed, the tenant obtained full vacant possession, various dates were settled (eg for rent review, break options, termination) and on the grant of the lease immediately thereafter the tenant acquired a real right and was thus able to fit out against that background of safety. However, it has now become commonplace, particularly in retail developments, to give the tenant access earlier than practical completion. Opinions differ about whether the pressure for earlier access arose because of tenants wishing to carry out fitting-out works and open earlier or because landlords wished by the application of this provision to reduce the length of rent-free periods. Whatever the genesis of these dates, they are now very common, albeit that they create certain problems:

(i)   The first such difficulty is that, unlike a certificate of practical completion, the phrase 'access certificate' or something similar has no technical meaning and many agreements define this date as that upon which the developer's architect (or other professional) issues a certificate to the effect that the works have reached such a state as will allow the tenant to commence its fitting-out works.

(ii)   Such undiluted drafting, particularly if the works refer only to the subjects of lease, might mean that the tenant was required to take access (if under such an obligation) or to start a rent-free period without a guarantee that the subjects of lease were wind and watertight, had services connected, could be reached by construction vehicles or were reasonably free of developer's contractors or indeed that there was an area (probably part of common parts) suitable for contractors' plant and equipment needed for fitting out. For that reason, most tenants impose criteria on the definition of the access date, including that the party issuing the certificate must reasonably expect to issue the certificate of practical completion within a few weeks, often four. The solicitors acting for both landlord and tenant should ensure that, if the specification contains detail on access criteria, these do not contradict the access criteria specified in the body of the agreement. One simple method of doing do is to set up a hierarchy of documents, such that the agreement is specifically stated to take precedence over any other document. Apart from ensuring that fitting out can proceed free of unreasonable interference, the tenant must avoid a delay in its projected opening date. Fitting out, hiring staff, advertising and (if retail) stocking up are very expensive. In industrial property the tenant may have installed, at considerable expense, items of very sophisticated machinery. If the developer fails timeously to issue the certificate of practical completion and the necessary approval of the building control authority cannot be given to enable the development to be opened to the public or to be staffed, the tenant who is prevented from trading has incurred a loss and may argue that in addition to an extension of any rent-free period equal to the precise period of delay, it is entitled to some compensation, possibly calculated by way of additional rent-free occupation.

(iii)   A further difficulty is that until the grant of the lease the tenant has a personal contract only and any expenditure incurred by that tenant on the property will merely form a claim for damages should the development not be completed and the lease not granted.

2.14 The method of triggering the date of entry by the issue of a certificate of practical completion is not itself entirely without difficulty. Developers wish an unqualified right to issue the certificate of practical completion when their professional adviser considers it appropriate and in support of that argument raise issues such as the obligation of the architect (or other relevant professional) in terms of the building contract. From a tenant's perspective, this is unpersuasive because the proper issue of the certificate can be separated from any such obligation. Major tenants therefore have no great difficulty in providing for a 'fast track' dispute procedure to be determined by a pre-named expert within a limited time, such expert to decide whether the certificate has been properly issued and for that exercise to be repeated until the expert is satisfied.

2.15 However, the advent of access dates renders this much less important. If the tenant has taken access and has completed an expensive fit-out, it is unlikely that it would wish to hold up the date of entry. The importance has shifted to the access date with its attendant difficulties of determination and the tenant should try to ensure the inclusion of a reference to an expert in determining the proper issue of the certificate of access.

2.16 With property already built, the date of entry to be inserted in the lease is agreed by the parties. In new developments it is usual for entry (as opposed to access) to be triggered by the certificate of practical completion. In modern shopping centres, this may be qualified in several ways. The developer, for reasons of publicity, may opt for a unified centre-opening date, although that can cause administrative problems. Most tenants would try to avoid entry/access occurring during the Christmas/New Year break and some major retail tenants have opening 'windows' which place the developer under pressure if unforeseen construction problems emerge; the developer should try to resist or at least limit the length of the periods during which the tenant can reject or delay handover.

2.17 Unless stated otherwise, rent starts on the date of entry. In practice, tenants are often given rent-free periods to reflect the need to fit out the property or as an incentive (for rent review implications, see paras 8.34–8.37), the details of which should be contained within the heads of terms. The lease usually proceeds on the basis of being income-producing from entry, so that the details of the rent-free period form a personal contract (contained in the agreement) between the developer (who may not be the same party as the landlord) and the tenant. Although this procedure contains an element of risk for the tenant, it is very common. Solicitors for each party should nevertheless pay particular regard to the definition of the rent commencement date. Changes to that definition are not unusual in complex negotiations involving access dates and the timing links to the date of entry (para 2.13) and the financial consequences of misunderstanding a client's instructions for a valuable property can be severe. It is rare (but not unknown) for the 'rent-free period' to relate to monetary payments other than rent. The landlord would expect service charge and insurance premiums to start on the access date, albeit for practical purposes at reduced levels.

'REPAIRING' CONSIDERATIONS

2.18 As will be seen in Chapter 5, the tenant is commonly expected to pay for all repairs, no matter how fundamental. If a problem emerges, the loss to the tenant may extend beyond the cost of remedying the defect to include substantial economic loss due to loss of trade, damage to equipment etc, not all of which may be recoverable from insurance; consequently, in the agreement, the tenant should consider ways of managing that risk, among which are the following:

2.19 Where the building already exists, a full structural survey should be considered; where the building is the whole or part of a development about to be constructed, procedures for regular inspection as mentioned in paragraph 2.12 are common. Nevertheless it remains impractical for tenants properly to survey major developments despite their potential liability for rebuilding costs through service charge. Indeed the task of managing the repairing risk has been made more difficult with the implementation on 14 July 2000 of the contaminated land regime under the Environmental Protection Act 1990, Pt IIA. That regime is somewhat restrictive, being based on the 'suitable for use' principle, and thereby leaving the planning system as the major control to deal with our industrial legacy. Nevertheless the statutory scheme could leave a tenant with responsibility for a very expensive remediation scheme and, unless the tenant can obtain an indemnity from the landlord (as opposed to the reverse), it would be prudent to bring contamination into the ambit of any pre-agreement survey. If, as part of a larger development, environmental surveys (and possibly work) have been carried out by the landlord, the tenant's advisers should inspect the reports, obtain confirmation from the consultants that all work has been completed satisfactorily and negotiate collateral warranties from those involved (para 2.26).

2.20 For existing buildings, and generally for leases of a short duration, the landlord may be prepared to agree to a schedule of condition (often photographic) being prepared by the tenant and annexed to the lease (para 5.18).

2.21 Major tenants may obtain significant relief from responsibility for latent defects (para 5.19) by either an indemnity from the developer or from the benefits of an insurance policy against the emergence of such a defect in the period of ten years following practical completion. Such a policy has the attractions to the tenant of avoiding any need to prove fault on the part of any consultant or contractor and being unrelated to their financial status, or indeed, existence. However, these major concessions to tenants are relatively rare and in the case of a decennial insurance policy need to be in contemplation prior to the start of construction to enable the advisers of the insurance company to conduct a thorough review of the procedures.

2.22 Usually, building contracts provide for a defects liability period of 12 months. The tenant's solicitor may wish to require that the landlord will procure that the contractor remedies all such defects timeously and with the minimum of inconvenience. The landlord's solicitor may wish specifically to require appropriate co-operation from the tenant.

2.23 However, in the scale of these various methods for managing the risks of major repair costs, one has outstripped all the others in its almost universal application and in the effort required, namely the provision to tenants of collateral warranties. A detailed examination of this subject is outwith the scope of this book but the following practical matters regularly engage the attention of parties in lease negotiations.

2.24 Because of the erosion during the 1980s of the ability to recover damages under delict[1] third parties found themselves unable to recover losses from construction team members unless they could demonstrate adequate proximity. Nor did *jus quaesitum tertio* provide an easy remedy because of difficulties in establishing an intention to confer the benefit[2], albeit that one wonders whether this could have been overcome in the terms of the contracts rather than turn to a method that seems to owe much to the English doctrine of privity of contract[3]. Accordingly, the creation of a contract running alongside the principal contracts governing building works created the necessary direct contractual duty.

---

1   See, for example, in England, *Murphy v Brentwood District Council* [1991] 1 AC 398.
2   *Strathford East Kilbride Ltd v HLM Design Ltd* 1999 SLT 121, 1997 SCLR 877.
3   See Macaulay and Wedderburn, 'Collateral Warranties – An Unnecessary Encumbrance' 1999 SLT (News) 23.

2.25 Collateral warranties are regarded by tenants (and purchasers) as an expectation, not an added extra. Accordingly, landlords (and their solicitors) engaging the professional team well in advance of any negotiations with tenants should address at that early stage the availability of collateral warranties in favour of purchasers and tenants and the detailed terms on offer. If, contrary to present practice, collateral warranties were not available to the tenants, the landlord would be limited to offering to the proposed tenants an obligation to pursue the relevant members of the professional team etc and that for inter alia the benefit of the tenants. Such a 'second best' option would be unlikely to be received by the tenants without concern.

2.26 Collateral warranties from all contractors, sub-contractors and professional team members might be ideal but impractical given the logistics of setting up their availability and procurement. Latent defects tend to emerge in design issues and the key players are those with a significant design role, such as the architect, engineer, mechanical and electrical engineer, quantity surveyor (in respect of prohibited materials), building contractor (and any specialist design sub-contractor), project manager and planning supervisor. The tenant should also obtain warranties from any consultants and contractors involved in any site investigations or reports into or works on contamination of the subjects of lease or the development of which they form a part (para 2.19).

2.27 The key components are:

- an expressed duty of care, similar to that enjoyed by the employer. But that duty is constrained by the function for which each team member has been engaged, hence the need for the tenant (and its advisers) to know the detailed terms of each letter of appointment (or, in the case of the building contractor, the building contract) to ensure that there is no shortfall;
- the duration is now commonly placed at between ten and twelve years;
- the tenant should be granted an irrevocable royalty-free non-exclusive licence to copy and use the relevant drawings subject to reimbursement of any photocopying costs;
- the team members and the contractor may try to 'cap' the financial exposure and exclude economic loss. From the tenant's angle, neither is ideal;
- the tenant is likely to take comfort from the availability of professional indemnity insurance and should insist on minimum levels of cover throughout the warranty period, although practical difficulties do exist including the prospect of the team member compromising or waiving the claim or vitiating the policy;

- as noted in paragraph 2.9, developers try to resist granting any obligation to avoid the use of prohibited materials, in which event the tenant should look for protection in the collateral warranties. Any such list should ideally include a 'sweeper' clause;

- contractors and team members usually insist on a net contribution clause whereby their liability is limited to an amount which would be reasonable on the assumption (if not a fact) that all other members had provided similar contractual undertakings;

- whether the benefits of such collateral warranties should be personal to the first tenant or capable of assignation is much debated although the current 'industry standard' appears to be two assignations;

- the tenant's solicitor should include in the agreement a clause to require the delivery of all signed warranties within a few weeks of entry and should ensure that this administrative matter is fulfilled timeously. The absence of collateral warranties which have been overlooked does cause difficulty.

2.28 Much time is spent by parties in the adjustment of collateral warranties and their related contracts. In current practice, they are routinely granted and expected and the landlord and its advisers should anticipate that requirement in their early discussions with the professional team. That said, tenants of property built some years ago may have to accept that no such comfort is available.

TENANT'S FITTING-OUT WORKS/COMMENCEMENT OF TRADE

2.29 A tenant taking the lease of a formerly occupied property will usually need to carry out some alterations prior to occupation. The lease will govern the precise basis upon which such alterations can be carried out (para 9.39) but it is sensible for the tenant's advisers to ensure that the landlord's approval to these initial works (without which the tenant could not trade) is granted (at least informally) prior to the agreement being signed. In the case of a tenant being provided with a developer's shell, the landlord's likely reaction to fitting-out proposals is simpler to judge and indeed part of the package may be a design guide. Although major tenants may resist, it is important to the developer that the tenant completes approved fitting-out proposals within a particular timeframe, the more so where a unified centre opening date is contemplated. It is common, therefore, for the agreement to require the tenant to submit a number of copies of plans and specifications fully displaying fitting-out proposals within a stated timescale preceding the access date and a requirement that the tenant should use all reasonable endeavours to obtain the necessary local authority consents. There are competing opinions about whether the developer's fees for approving the tenant's fitting-out proposals should be paid by the tenant. The tenant would argue that this is a developer's cost. The developer can become rightly annoyed if its adviser's fees are increased due to inadequately advanced proposals. There are two ancillary documents that are relevant, namely:

(i)   a fitting-out licence, a draft of which will be annexed to the agreement and to the executed version of which will be attached in due course the agreed plans and specifications. A licence will conventionally contain obligations upon the tenant as to the standard of construction required, the need for compliance with statutory regulations (including the Construction (Design and Management) Regulations 1994), the provision of insurance information (which the tenant should limit to the cost, not value, of fitting-out works, thereby avoiding being involved in any valuation exercise for insurance purposes), the production of statutory consents and written notice when all is complete. Reinstatement provisions at termination may in some circumstances from a tenant's perspective require modification on whether the landlord has an absolute or qualified right, relative time periods and the impact on rent review; and

(ii)   in shopping centres, a tenant's guide. This is a detailed document advising the tenant of the means by which men, materials and vehicles are allowed access to the centre, provisions if any for access to the mall etc, all with a view to ensuring a sensible fitting-out programme for all tenants which would minimise inconvenience or disturbance and allow some units to trade while others are being fitted out. This is a practical document whose details should be considered not just by the solicitor acting for the tenant but also by its surveyor. The solicitor should, however, ensure that there is not, as in some centres, an obligation upon the tenant to comply with the terms of the tenant's guide as the same may be changed from time to time at the discretion of the developer. While the possibility of change has to be recognised, some objective standards should be set.

2.30 At the end of the fitting-out period there is frequently in the agreement an obligation upon the tenant to occupy physically or, in the case of retail, to commence trading within a particular timescale. Although some tenants try to resist, such a clause is important to the landlord in a multi-occupancy building, particularly in the retail sector, and vital where some tenants may have negotiated rental discounts until a proportion of the centre is open and trading. The obligation of continuous occupation is considered at paragraphs 9.34–9.38.

GRANT OF LEASE

2.31 The agreement provides for the mechanics of the grant of the lease. If the subjects are not then built, the various dates in the lease, for example entry, termination, rent review, will all depend on formulae in the agreement. The date of entry is considered in paragraphs 2.13–2.17 but the clause dealing with the grant itself should refer to the duration and the rent review pattern. Both parties wish to ensure that the lease is granted quickly. As already discussed in paragraph 2.2, agreements often contain provisions debarring the tenant from alienating the agreement and the tenant should opt to treat such a provision as *pro non scripto* if the landlord does not adhere to a realistic timescale for execution. Further, although leases of a duration not exceeding 20 years result in the tenant acquiring on entry a real right on the execution of the agreement, that is not so where land registration is relevant. Lastly, of course, any requirement to borrow money on security of the lease would demand immediate recording or registration. Because of the delays in the Land Register it has become common to provide for dual registration in the Books of Council and Session and in the Land Register.

BACK LETTERS

2.32 The need for and scope of any back letters becomes clear during the negotiation of the detailed terms of the lease and parties should remember to include in the agreement a short clause which will trigger the execution of any back letter, usually simultaneously with execution of the lease.

2.33 The original objective of a back letter was to dilute or waive for the benefit of the original tenant alone an obligation which in terms of the lease would fall upon that tenant and its successors. There is little risk in this procedure if the subject matter is limited to, say, a waiver of the obligation to insure plate glass. But, increasingly, back letters are being used to qualify fundamentally important conditions of the lease (eg, 'keep open', repairs, service charge cap, rent-free period) or commercial arrangements such as exclusivity. If any important issues are to be included in a back letter, the solicitors for both parties need to be clear about the intention, decide if a back letter is a suitable vehicle and draft it with care and precision.

2.34 If the only reason for a back letter is to limit concessions to the original tenant, a clause in the lease suitably drafted would achieve that purpose. But landlords prefer that concessions extracted for individual tenants in specific market conditions should remain out of public gaze, in respect of negotiations for either future lettings or on rent reviews. Accordingly, personal concessions, although not uncommon in leases, are much more frequently found in back letters.

2.35 In accepting a personal concession in a back letter, the tenant's solicitor should ensure that his/her client's interests are not immediately defeated by an early sale of the landlord's interest. If the back letter covers any important issue it must incorporate a clause obliging the granter to take a purchaser bound to grant a new back letter in identical terms, a matter that seems to have been overlooked for the tenant in *Optical Express (Gyle) Ltd v Marks & Spencer plc*[1]. Landlords may try to dilute this to an obligation to use reasonable endeavours.

---

1   *Optical Express (Gyle) Ltd v Marks & Spencer plc* 2000 SLT 644.

2.36 Back letters about commercially important matters have the potential for difficulty. Among the problems are:

(i)   if a back letter is written in terms which amount to a variation of the lease, it could have important results. Such a back letter which requires, for example, the tenant to pay a rent greater than open market rent would fall within the purview of the rent review surveyor and be susceptible to arguments about its discounting effect on rent review;

(ii)   if not a variation, successor landlords are not bound by its terms, even if, as decided in *Allan v Armstrong*[1], they are aware of its existence, and failure by a landlord to comply with an obligation to require its successor to grant a new back letter gives to the tenant no rights against the successor. An action years later against the original granter of the back letter may be fruitless;

(iii)   a back letter can easily become detached from the extract lease;

(iv)   costs are incurred producing new ones on each occasion that the landlord disposes of its interest.

---

1   2004 GWD 37–768.

EXCLUSIVITY CLAUSES

2.37 The heads of terms may, usually in a retail development, include exclusivity for the tenant, complete or limited, in respect of its use or part of it. Paragraph 10.8 deals with the impact of the Competition Act 1998 (Land Agreements Exclusion Revocation) Order 2010 and time will tell how far this impacts on such clauses. For so long as these clauses remain in use, the respective solicitors need clarity on their clients' understanding of the terms 'agreed', certainly in respect of these matters:

- Is this a personal undertaking by the developer or is it to bind successive landlords? If the former, the tenant should be told that it could be deprived of any advantage by an early sale of the landlord's interest. If the latter, the developer needs to be relaxed about the likely attitude of a prospective purchaser of the investment and the clause must be included in the lease, not in the agreement. A back letter is also an unhelpful vehicle (para 2.36).

- Is it to be personal to the tenant, as is common? If not so, the tenant may consider that it has an advantage but may pay the penalty if faced with an argument about a premium rent on review (para 8.43).

- What are the precise uses to which the exclusive right applies and how many (if any) other tenants are allowed to trade in that range of uses?

- Can the developer implement such an obligation, given the user clauses appearing in agreements for lease already signed? In this respect the landlord's solicitor must have regard to the prospect of any other tenant deciding to alter its product range within its authorised user clause which in some cases may be an Open Class 1 User.

The landlord's solicitor, having negotiated an exclusivity clause, then requires to ensure that no subsequent agreements are concluded in terms that could leave the landlord open to a breach of contract and in pursuance of that objective must specifically prohibit the exclusive uses in future leases.

EXPENSES

2.38 Save by agreement to the contrary, the tenant will be responsible for stamp duty land tax and registration dues but, as will be well known to practitioners in the field, it is often the case that tenants are requested also to pay the landlord's reasonable legal expenses. This is not a system attended by much common sense but, if the tenant has to pay, the sum should be agreed prior to the agreement being executed, as should the date of payment. It is fairly common for 50 per cent (sometimes 75 per cent) to be paid on execution of the agreement and the rest when the lease is granted. This is a clause that should appear in the agreement, leaving any expenses clause in the lease to deal only with stamp duty land tax and registration dues.

VALUE ADDED TAX

2.39 Since 1989, VAT has been charged on the construction of commercial property. The granting of leases is generally exempt but carries the disadvantage of the inability of the landlord to recover input tax. The landlord can overcome this on an individual property basis by opting to tax (formerly known as electing to waive the exemption) thereby charging VAT on both rents and any future sales proceeds. Such a decision is irrevocable although a successor owner is not bound and can treat the supply as exempt. Whether a tenant or purchaser would be concerned at being charged VAT depends on their VAT status. A tenant may well want to ensure that the landlord who is charging VAT on the rent is indeed registered for VAT and has made the appropriate election. In considering whether to exercise the option to tax the landlord should be given specialist tax advice.

2.40 However, one general matter merits discussion here, namely inducements. Those that relate to assignations and renunciations are mentioned in Chapter 12 but an agreement to lease may provide for a payment by the tenant to the landlord or vice versa. Where the tenant is paying, the supply is exempt subject to the landlord's option to tax. A situation where the landlord paid the tenant was considered in the *Mirror Group* case[1] where Customs argued that the payments were consideration for a standard rated supply of services by the tenant. The European Court disagreed. A taxable person who only paid the consideration in respect of a supply of services did not itself make a supply. However a taxable supply might be identified exceptionally where the tenant was perceived as an anchor tenant, thereby providing advertising services. This decision was followed by a narrow interpretation of the relevant paragraph of that judgement by the High Court[2] and, mindful of the dubiety which had been created, HM Revenue and Customs issued guidance in the form of Business Brief 04/03, as replaced by Business Brief 12/05, which confirms that inducement payments are mainly outside the scope of VAT and are only a taxable consideration when directly linked to a specific benefit supplied by a tenant to a landlord. Examples given include the carrying out by the tenant of upgrading or improvement works which are actually the landlord's responsibility and which it is paying the tenant to carry out or, as in the *Mirror Group* case, the tenant acting as anchor tenant.

---

1   *Commissioners of Customs and Excise v Mirror Group plc* [2001] ECR I-7175, [2001] STC 1453, ECJ.
2   *Trinity Mirror plc (formerly Mirror Group plc) v Customs and Excise Commissioners* 2003 EWHC 480 (Ch), [2003] STC 518.

MISCELLANEOUS

2.41 All agreements will contain clauses on some of the following matters:

2.42 It is essential that the tenant be satisfied that the subjects of lease have been erected in accordance with all required statutory consents and that planning permission exists for the tenant's use on terms acceptable to the tenant. The landlord will not usually provide any guarantee that the property can lawfully be used for the tenant's required use, and the lease will often make specific reference to there being no such warranty by the landlord. It is vital that the tenant checks this carefully. Further comments on this and the consequences of failure to do so are contained at paragraphs 7.13 and 9.33. Where the agreement relates to a development not yet built, these matters are likely to be governed by suspensive conditions such as are discussed at paragraph 2.5 and by the obligations mentioned in paragraph 2.9. When the subjects of lease already exist, the tenant should include a clause requiring the landlord to provide the usual form of local searches, including a copy of the extant planning permission.

2.43 Where the tenant is taking a lease of the whole (or a major part) of the development, it is reasonable for the tenant to require the landlord to produce by the date of entry a full set of 'as-built' drawings and the necessary manuals for the operation of all plant and equipment.

2.44 For existing properties, the tenant is also likely to require exhibition of an asbestos audit for the property to ensure that the statutory requirements[1] (which will become the tenant's responsibility) have been complied with prior to the date of entry.

---

1   Control of Asbestos at Work Regulations 2002 and the Control of Asbestos Regulations 2006.

2.45 The landlord should be required to produce the usual local authority searches for existing buildings and, even in new developments, parties need to ensure that all consents are in place, including road construction consents, to enable access to be obtained from the public road network.

2.46 A coal mining report will be necessary in some areas as identified by the Law Society.

2.47 A general procedure for service of notices is common and a similar provision will appear in the lease. Indeed in the latter case, there may be formal notices required for irritancy, break options, rent reviews, dilapidations and termination. Each of these will be considered in relation to individual topics but the general clause, both in the agreement and the lease, is likely to require service by recorded delivery to the registered office of the intended recipient (if a company) or otherwise to the premises or the last known address. Usually a notice is deemed served after two days from posting unless the contrary can be proved. This form of clause does not usually provoke dispute but the procedure will not be mandatory unless so stated. Due to the inherent dangers in the service of notices to the subjects of lease, there is a clear case for mandatory procedures.

2.48 Given that parties to Scottish leases are regularly based in England, it is helpful to refer to Scots law and to have parties prorogate the jurisdiction of the courts here.

STAMP DUTY LAND TAX

2.49 The Finance Act 2003 introduced Stamp Duty Land Tax ('SDLT') in place of the previous stamp duty regime. The old system had been a tax payable only on deeds which were to be registered. The current system is a tax on property transactions, whether or not the deed evidencing that transaction requires to be registered. SDLT on a lease is due by the tenant with the amount of tax payable being based on the rent payable over the length of the lease (less a discount – see para 2.53), plus any premium being paid by the tenant to the landlord.

2.50 The type of agreement for lease considered in this chapter (ie a contract, followed by the grant of a formal lease) does not, *per se*, trigger any SDLT payment. However, it will contain a requirement for the tenant's solicitor to submit an SDLT return (SDLT 1) and to pay the SDLT due within a specified period of time after the effective date (para 2.55). The statutory period allowed for submission of the SDLT 1 and payment of the tax due is 30 days from the effective date but submission and production of the submission receipt (SDLT 5) is likely to be required by the landlord within 14 days of the effective date. The lease cannot be registered without the SDLT 5 being produced. In practice, the tenant's solicitor should send the SDLT 1, along with a request for the funds to pay the SDLT to the tenant as soon as the effective date is known (see para 2.55), to ensure compliance with the statutory time limits and those set out in the agreement.

2.51 The agreement may set out other clauses specific to the SDLT 1; in particular, landlords often require that the form is completed so as to ensure that the SDLT certificate is sent to the solicitor rather than to the premises. Currently online submission of the form does not allow this, although in practice an electronic version of the form is sent to the submitting solicitor.

2.52 No submission is required for Leases with a duration of less than 7 years where no tax would be payable. A lease of more than seven years will require an SDLT 1 to be submitted even if no tax is actually payable unless:

- any chargeable consideration, other than rent, is less than £40,000; and
- the Annual Rent is less than £1,000.

2.53 The amount of SDLT due is based on the 'net present value' of the rent (including VAT if appropriate) payable over the full duration of the lease, less a 'temporal discount rate', currently 3.5% per annum. The tax is calculated by applying the relevant percentage (currently 1%) to the excess of the net present value over the appropriate threshold (currently £150,000). Any premium paid by the tenant for the grant of the lease is chargeable to SDLT. However a reverse premium (payable by the landlord to the tenant) is not. The HMRC website contains a useful calculator which allows the calculation to be made quickly and easily. If the rent is uncertain as at the effective date (for example if a turnover rent is payable) a reasonable estimate requires to be made of the rent payable for the first five years and the submission based on that. A further submission would require to be made after 5 years. There are detailed provisions in the legislation regarding variations to the rent within the first five years of the duration, and 'abnormal rent increases' outwith the first five years and the need to submit further returns in that regard.

2.54 In calculating the rent payable, it should be noted:

- Any rent free period will reduce the amount of rent payable so the rent for that period will be treated as being zero.

- If VAT is chargeable on the rent, it is the VAT inclusive figure that is to be used. If VAT was not chargeable at the outset of the Lease, the fact that the Landlord subsequently waives its VAT exemption does not trigger any additional SDLT.

- If the rent is increased in line with the Retail Prices Index, the effect of any such increase is ignored for SDLT purposes.

2.55 SDLT becomes due on the effective date. The question of what is the effective date is far from simple. In cases such as the ones considered in this chapter generally, where an agreement for lease is entered into prior to the grant of the lease, it is the date of substantial performance of the contract that will be the effective date. This will usually be the date when the tenant takes entry to the premises, notwithstanding the date on which the lease is actually signed. As such, solicitors acting for a tenant should ensure that they are kept informed of when entry is being taken given the requirement to submit the SDLT return, and to pay the tax due, which flows from that.

2.56 The legislation allows for reliefs to be claimed for certain transactions. Those most likely to be encountered involve charities, dealings between related companies and the leaseback element of a sale and leaseback transaction. Care needs to be taken with any reliefs claimed and attention paid to the possibility of a change in circumstances after the effective date which might result in the subsequent withdrawal of relief and a resultant charge to tax.

2.57 The tax is also payable on assignations and renunciations where a premium is payable and is calculated on the amount of that premium, with no account being taken of the level of rent payable under the lease. However, if the original grant of the lease was exempt from SDLT, unless the assignation itself qualifies for a relief, an assignation of the tenant's interest would be treated as the grant of a lease and SDLT will be payable on the rent payable for the unexpired duration of the lease. It should also be noted that reverse premia are not chargeable to SDLT.

2.58 Finally, it should be noted that the Scotland Bill and Command Paper published on 30 November 2010 provides for the complete devolution of SDLT. This would mean the current system being replaced by a specific Scottish tax, the details of which will be determined by the Scottish Parliament, although no change is expected before 2015.

ARBITRATION

2.59 Many agreements (and leases, both generally and in respect of rent review) contain arbitration clauses. The private nature of arbitration has contributed to the historic absence of Scottish authority on various points of law. The Arbitration (Scotland) Act 2010 now governs arbitrations in Scotland and, in repealing Section 3 of the Administration of Justice Act 1972, has effectively removed the ability of parties to state a case on a point of law, a provision which was widely seen as undermining the whole purpose of arbitration.

GREEN ISSUES

2.60 In terms of the Energy Performance of Buildings (Scotland) Regulations 2008[1] which implemented Article 4(3) of Directive 2002/91/ EC of the European Parliament, an energy performance certificate ('EPC') is to be produced when a building is sold or leased. The term 'building' is defined in Article 2 of the Directive. EPCs are produced by accredited assessors and must measure energy performance calculated and expressed in accordance with an approved methodology. The owner or, where the owner is not the occupier, the occupier of a public building (one with a floor area exceeding 1000m2 occupied by a public authority or by a body providing public services and which can be visited by the public) must display a similar certificate (the Display Energy Certificate, or 'DEC') prominently in the building. Parties engaged in a relevant transaction need to provide for the production of an EPC and, in the case of a 'public building', to verify the proper display of the DEC. To date, agreements do not generally demand any minimum standard to be disclosed in the EPC; the mere production of the certificate tends to suffice.

---

1   No 309 as amended by 389

Chapter 3

The Subjects of Lease

THE SUBJECTS

3.1 Clarity is essential on the extent of the subjects of lease, the larger subjects of which they form part, and any rights and reservations. Any ambiguity can lead to difficulties not just of possession but in respect of, for example, liability for repairs or impact upon rent review.

3.2 In some cases the task of the draftsman is not materially different from that when framing a disposition in a feudal title and the same drafting techniques apply. In the case of a lease to be registered in the Land Register the description must be sufficient to enable the Keeper to identify the premises with reference to an Ordnance Survey plan. Because of their nature and, in particular, the inclusion of rent review clauses, leases are frequently considered in detail by management surveyors and those which contain descriptions reliant themselves on a feudal title and without a plan create management difficulties. Where the landlord is letting part of what is contained in its feudal title then a clear description of the extent of the subjects of lease is vital.

3.3 In practice, many modern commercial leases cannot derive assistance from the property title for the framing of any description of the premises, because the extent of the property to be let is dictated not by a consideration of its physical dimensions but by the control which the landlord considers to be essential for the management of its investment. A clear understanding by both parties and their advisers of what is the direct responsibility of the tenant or of the landlord is crucial to a proper appreciation of many clauses in the lease, of which the most important are the repairing and insuring clauses, service charge and rent review.

3.4 There are broadly three types of situation.

(i)   If the landlord is leasing all that it owns then it would usually choose to lease the structure, probably by reference to the property title.

(ii)   At the other extreme, modern office blocks or shopping centres are extremely sophisticated. For obvious management reasons, to lease these items in common to individual tenants would reduce landlord flexibility and control to an unacceptable level. In such cases the landlord retains not only common unbuilt-on areas but the main structure, foundations etc of the whole development. Accordingly, the subjects leased to individual tenants will extend only to interior plasterwork and be little more than a lease of airspace. Lest it be thought that by this device of increasing control the landlord is enlarging its exposure to repairing costs, it will be appreciated that by the use of sophisticated service charge provisions, total liability remains that of the various tenants.

(iii)   There are many leases in the middle ground, such as in retail parks, where each individual lease includes the roof and main structure of the individual unit and a right in common to mutual walls with unbuilt-on areas such as car parking and landscaping (and often the canopy) remaining with the landlord, who retrieves the maintenance costs through service charge.

FIXTURES

3.5 The relevance of fixtures to the obligations of the parties on matters such as repairs, rent review and removal rights can make it important to be clear about the distinction between a moveable item (to which repairing obligations do not apply) on the one hand and a fixture (a heritable item) on the other, and in the latter case whether it is a landlord's fixture or a tenant's fixture. In *Scottish Discount Company Ltd v Blin*[1] it was held that the proper tests to determine if an item was a fixture included:

- whether, and if so, to what degree the item is attached to the subjects of lease but, importantly, not to the exclusion of other relevant elements;

- whether the attachment was of a permanent or quasi permanent nature;

- whether its removal would destroy the item or the subjects of lease;

- to what extent would the use of the subjects of lease be affected by the removal;

- whether the building was adapted specifically for the use of the item;

- the intention of the party who had attached the item ascertained from the item and building and the nature of the attachment, not from extrinsic evidence.

Each case needs to be determined on its individual circumstances but where an item is judged to be a fixture, it can belong to either the landlord or the tenant.

1   *Scottish Discount Company Ltd v Blin* 1985 SC 216, 1986 SLT 123.

3.6 The landlord's fixtures will include items already attached to the subjects of lease at the date of the tenant's entry and those affixed thereafter by either party in accordance with the provisions of the lease, unless these comprise items installed by the tenant for its business purposes not prohibited by the lease and capable of being removed without irreparable damage to the subjects of lease. Such tenant's fixtures will be part of the subjects of lease and thereby fall within the repairing obligations, including those at termination. However the tenant can remove the fixtures at any time, including at termination, subject to making good damage thereby caused.

3.7 To reduce the uncertainty inherent in these matters, the safest course for the landlord is to include within the definition of the subjects of lease all additions (except tenants' fixtures and fittings), alterations and improvements and all the landlord's fixtures and fittings. That method confirms ownership and places these items within the tenant's repairing obligations. In the removal clause the landlord can require (a) the surrender of the subjects of lease (which by definition includes the landlord's fixtures and fittings), (b) that any missing or damaged items are replaced, and (c) that the tenant pays for any damage caused in the removal of the tenant's fixtures and fittings. These provisions are usually agreed without difficulty but the tenant should in this matter be aware of the rent review implications. All work which the tenant carries out to the subjects of lease has to be considered in the context of the alterations clause (paras 9.39–9.46). If consent is required, the tenant should try to avoid the licence for works providing that the works are to be reinstated or left, whichever the landlord wishes in its absolute discretion. To some extent the final agreement will be dependent on the kind of work or the nature of the fixtures and fittings which are being contemplated.

COMMON RIGHTS

3.8 The tenant will require, in addition to a lease of the subjects, certain other rights and it is preferable from the tenant's point of view if these are stated expressly, rather than reliance placed upon common law duties of the landlord to provide essential rights to the tenant such as rights of support and protection where the subjects of lease are part of a larger building. The extent of these rights, common and sole, is site-specific, and dependent upon the nature of the lease. In all cases, clarity of drafting is necessary. In *Marfield Properties Ltd v Secretary of State for the Environment*[1], the court held that the phrase 'common parts' was not a term of art and required to be interpreted by the ordinary rules. In that case 'all other parts' which were common included the roof. Among the points that may be considered are:

---

1   *Marfield Properties v Secretary of State for the Environment* 1996 SC 362, 1996 SLT 1244.

3.9 In the form of lease described in paragraph 3.4 (ii) the 'common parts' or some such similar phrase is utilised to describe all parts of the development as constructed which do not form part of the various lettable units. Because these lettable units exclude structure it follows that the common parts will include the whole structure of the development. The landlord will grant a series of common rights to use, with others, the common parts subject to such regulations as the landlord prescribes (paragraph 3.17). Those representing the tenant should ensure that these common rights include all physical access rights that are necessary for staff, customers and service vehicles, rights for transmitters, rights to use any car park and rights to enable the tenant to comply with all its obligations in terms of the lease, such as repairs which could require access over adjoining subjects. Particular care must be taken to ensure that the tenant has access (whether or not in common with others) to the public road network. In industrial estates, many internal roads are private and access rights over them are necessary for the tenant of any unit in the estate.

3.10 In closed or partially closed centres in particular the question of the hours during which the tenant must have a right of access for trading purposes over such as malls, access ways, escape corridors and the like requires to be settled, as does the need to fix availability of service roads, corridors, bays and lifts for delivery purposes with such rights being qualified from the perspective of the landlord by the need to ensure that these elements are used by the tenant so as to avoid obstructions. The trading hours of some tenants, e.g. leisure operators, will not coincide with the retailers and the access arrangements will need to reflect the physical layout of the development. Service charge considerations come into play (para 6.32). The question of the hours that the landlord may wish to require all tenants to trade (often called 'core trading hours') is considered in paragraph 9.36 in the context of 'keep open' provisions.

3.11 Some tenants wish to ensure the availability of a connection into a common communication system for televisions and computers or, failing that, rights in principle to install their own in which latter case, depending on the nature of the development, the need for the landlord and any other owners in the development to consent to the detail needs to be considered. With an eye to future assignations and despite technological advances making this of declining importance, all tenants may be advised to ensure the inclusion of these rights even if their current business does not dictate any concern.

3.12 Retail developments in particular often have store directories at their entrances and, if such is to be provided, the tenant should be included; sometimes the relative size and placing of each entry can be an issue.

EXCEPTIONS AND RESERVATIONS

3.13 The tenant's right to possession of the whole subjects of lease and, if relevant, the grant to the tenants generally of rights to use common parts place an onus on the landlord's solicitor to reserve all rights necessary to manage the investment and indeed it is in the interests of the generality of tenants that no single tenant or small group of tenants is able to frustrate proper management. In *Possfund Custodian Trustee Ltd v Kwik-Fit Properties Ltd*[1] it was held that the meaning of a reservations clause was to be interpreted by reference to the intention of the parties at the time of the lease being granted and the form of environmental underground investigation there proposed by the landlord had not been in contemplation and could not be undertaken. Under explanation that such reservations and rights may be scattered and repeated through the lease, the following are issues requiring consideration:

---

1   *Possfund Custodian Trustee Ltd v Kwik-Fit Properties Ltd* 2009 SLT 133.

3.14 Paragraph 2.11 considered the needs of the developer to vary the initial layout of the development and the drafting implications for the agreement. Ideally, however, the landlord wishes throughout the duration of the various leases to be entitled:

(i)   to make physical changes within the footprint of the development originally contemplated. In a retail park, by a reservation of rights to vary, extend or reduce the common parts, the landlord could add units (eg a fast food outlet) or reduce the number. This legitimate expectation on the part of the landlord to add units would be matched by the tenant requiring that the common parts would continue to produce no less beneficial facilities at no materially greater liability;

(ii)   the ability of the landlord to reduce unit numbers causes concerns for the tenant whose agreed rent may reflect the footfall of a larger retail park of a particular layout and whose service charge, after proportional adjustment, may increase. In practice many landlords accept that a unit reduction is unlikely and will not pursue such a right;

(iii)   to extend the development outside its existing boundary. This may
be achieved either by a specific right or by a general reservation
supported by a definition of 'development' (or the equivalent)
relying on 'as existing from time to time'. The acquisition
of minor rights on the fringes of a development or even the
construction of another phase on identified land is probably
acceptable to many tenants but tenants should recognise that any
construction works (even if service charge excludes the capital
cost) may become common parts for the 'repair' of which tenants
are liable in service charge without the comfort of collateral
warranties. Tenants usually try to identify the possible tolerances
for the development on a plan and so limit the definition.

3.15 The landlord needs the right to take entry to the subjects of lease
for any legitimate purpose, including inspection and repair of the subjects
(on failure by the tenant) or the development, including where necessary
replacing, renewing or adding to transmitters serving other parts of the
development. This, from the landlord's perspective, is essential. Tenants
focus on requiring the landlord to act prudently by giving proper notice
(except in an emergency), taking entry only if no practicable alternative
exists, avoiding where possible the best trading period (if retail), restoring
damage and causing the least practicable inconvenience. The case of
William Collins & Sons Ltd v CGU Insurance plc[1] shows the need for
clarity on the extent and timing of the landlord's rights of entry. The
interest in this case does not lie in its outcome (it was remitted back to the
Outer House for further procedure) but that a landlord wanted to carry out
major repair works close to the lease termination date that would be highly
disruptive to the business of the tenant and would result in the landlord
extracting maximum value from the service charge provisions prior to
the lease expiry. That such an outcome was possible would suggest the
need for the reservations clause to be qualified. Reservations which go
so far as to allow the landlord to undermine, underpin and shore up the
subjects of lease, or build on to or over them would normally be regarded
as unnecessary but in the context of a shopping centre may have to be
considered in a diluted form. In any event the tenant should provide that
light and air to the subjects of lease are not to be reduced and that the
landlord makes good all damage caused to the subjects of lease and the

fixtures, fittings and stock, although that latter element is frequently debated.

---

1   2006 SC 674.

3.16 In the course of the lease, the landlord may have to alter or even close pedestrian and vehicular access routes or car parking arrangements, temporarily or permanently. Tenants would want to ensure that at all times adequate arrangements were in place, any disruption was minimised and any permanent changes did not materially and adversely affect the subjects of lease. Retailers are particularly nervous about access or car parking arrangements changing footfall. To close an access in a covered shopping centre to enable further development could be fatal to a tenant's trading position.

3.17 'Regulations' may be needed for the better management of the development. Provided that regulations are expressed to be confined to 'housekeeping' matters, not to deprive the tenant of rights granted and to be exercised in the interests of the generality of tenants, there is no problem with this.

Chapter 4

The Letting

4.1 Most leases narrate the letting itself immediately after the initial clause dealing with definitions and interpretation. The components include the parties, the duration, the initial rent and other financial liabilities, and there is brought into play the subjects of lease et cetera discussed in Chapter 3, often accompanied by the inclusion here of a clause to overcome the implied warranty by the landlord as to the fitness of the subject of lease. This latter point is discussed in paragraph 5.4.

THE PARTIES

4.2 As mentioned in paragraph 2.2, the developer who entered into the agreement for lease with the tenant may dispose of its interest at or prior to entry. The tenant's solicitor should carry out a proper examination of title to ensure inter alia that the lease is granted by the party infeft in the subjects or in right of the tenant's interest in a superior lease. Particular care should be taken by both parties to identify companies by their registered number.

4.3 The landlord's solicitor will wish to ensure that the party whose covenant was investigated by the landlord prior to the agreement is the same party that executes the lease, not, for example, another (but less substantial) company within the tenant group. The landlord needs also to control the identity of the tenant throughout the lease. The following elements are usually featured in the letting clause, associated with definitions and interpretation provisions:

- At common law a tenant of unfurnished urban subjects (with which this book is solely concerned) has an implied right to assign or sub-let. Landlords must exclude that right save in controlled circumstances. The terms of modern alienation clauses are very detailed and the letting clause should simply exclude all assignees and sub-tenants except where permitted in terms of the lease, leaving that detail for the alienation clause usually to be found under the tenant's general obligations.

- Leases to traditional partnerships, as opposed to limited liability partnerships, are fraught with difficulty. Questions about what constitutes dissolution, whether that terminates the lease or indeed whether changes in membership alone provoke termination do not admit of easy answers[1]. From a practical standpoint, the preferred course is to state the intention in the lease. It is common, both in respect of a lease to a partnership or to ensure maximum protection if a future tenant comprises a partnership, to state that the tenant comprises, jointly and severally, all the partners at the date of entry, their executors and all future partners. The tenant's solicitor should require that the landlord acts reasonably in considering a future request for release by a retiring or resigning partner or the executors of a deceased partner.

- Some leases require the tenant (sometimes only the original tenant) to be liable jointly and severally with the person from time to time vested in the tenant's interest (see also para 4.14). This approach has its origins in the English doctrine of privity of contract, itself affected by the Landlord and Tenant (Covenants) Act 1995 which does not apply to Scotland. Tenants should resist a joint and several obligation and ensure that any definition of the tenant which encompasses its successors refers to these being in substitution for it.

---

1   See *Inland Revenue Commissioners v Graham's Trustees* 1971 SC (HL)1; *Lujo Properties Ltd v Green* 1997 SLT 225; *Moray Estates Development Co v Butler* 1999 SLT 1338; *Knapdale (Nominees) Ltd v Donald* 2000 GWD 19–730, *Hisket v Wilson* 2003 GWD 38–1036 (OH).

4.4 If the covenant of the tenant is unacceptable to the landlord, the tenant may have offered a guarantor, whether a more substantial group company, the directors of the private tenant company or even an unrelated party in which event the guarantor will be a party to the lease, with the relative provisions often being contained in a schedule. Some guarantees are found in separate documents, triggered by an agreement for lease. The landlord will, as part of the exercise in relation to the tenant, investigate the covenant of the guarantor including, if a company, its ability to grant a guarantee and its domicile due to possible enforceability concerns with companies registered outwith the United Kingdom.

4.5 In settling the terms of the guarantee, one fundamental matter requires resolution, namely its duration. The following need addressed:

- a guarantor (who is likely to be a party connected to the tenant) expects its liability to relate to the identified tenant and thereby cease (i) on entry of a permitted assignee or (ii) in respect of liabilities arising subsequent to the demise of that tenant. On the matter at (i), the guarantor's expectations would be frustrated by either the form of guarantee that explicitly preserves liability 'on the transfer of the tenant's interest' or (but less obviously) by a definition of the tenant that includes successors and assignees or by the tenant's acceptance of a joint and several liability (para 4.3). On the matter at (ii), the loss to the landlord of the guarantee that would be caused by the demise of the tenant (by events such as personal bankruptcy or the striking off of a company) is often overcome by drafting that provides for a continuation of the guarantee and/or requires the guarantor to accept a new lease for the unexpired duration at the then current rent as reviewed but otherwise on the original terms. Guarantors prepared to accept this onerous obligation should impose a time limit from the relevant event within which any such demand must be made by the landlord. Accordingly, to the extent that any of these suggested provisions are unacceptable to the proposed guarantor, revisals need to be negotiated. It is difficult for landlords to resist drafting changes whose purpose is to limit the guarantee to the obligations of the original tenant which in ordinary circumstances would terminate on an assignation permitted under the alienation provisions (para 9.14).

- occasionally the guarantor will try to provide for the fall of a guarantee on a change, not just of the tenant, but of the landlord, a situation with clear dangers for the landlord. Success on the part of the guarantor is dependant on very clear drafting[1].

- a guarantee may be expressed to endure for a fixed period or until the tenant can demonstrate an appropriate covenant by the production of accounts for an agreed period of years disclosing pre-agreed profit levels or assets relative to rent. A test commonly used in the market is that of profits for each of three consecutive years reaching three times the rent.

- the liquidation or receivership of or the appointment of an administrator to the guarantor (if a company) or the bankruptcy or death of an individual guarantor is a justified concern for the landlord who may add these events to the triggers for invoking the irritancy clause, albeit that such a non-monetary breach invokes the concept of the 'fair and reasonable landlord' (para 11.8). Tenants will argue that they would be automatically deprived of a valuable lease by an event of which they had neither notice nor control. Parties sometimes agree a period for the tenant to produce a substitute guarantor acceptable to the landlord (who might accept the need to act reasonably), failing which the tenant would be in breach. Such a clause would remove the need for liquidation etc of the guarantor to be an irritancy event.

---

1   *Waydale Ltd v DHL Holdings (UK) Ltd (No 3)* 2001 SLT 224.

4.6 After settlement of the questions arising from the intended duration of the guarantee, including those related to changes in the identities of the parties, there are the following matters to consider:

- a general guarantee clause will leave the guarantor contingently liable for all and any obligations of the tenant. Some will limit this to rent and other monetary liabilities.

- the landlord will wish to retain its rights despite giving time to or failing to take action against the tenant and precise drafting is needed for that purpose[1].

- the guarantor would be discharged on a variation of the lease[2] so guarantees state otherwise. However the guarantor would be wise to limit this to non-material variations.

---

1   *Aitken's Trustees v Bank of Scotland* 1944 SC 270, 1945 SLT 84.
2   *N G Napier Ltd v Crosbie* 1964 SC 129, 1964 SLT 185 (1 DIV).

4.7 To provide for the guarantor the ability to take early action, the landlord should be required to advise the guarantor if the tenant is late in making rental payments and to serve upon the guarantor copies of all notices, formal or informal, sent by the landlord to the tenant. If the difficulty reaches the stage where the guarantor is required by the landlord to make any payment, that guarantor should have the right to demand from the tenant an assignation of the tenant's interest, leaving the guarantor able to dispose of that interest subject to the alienation provisions.

4.8 Even if the covenant of the original tenant is substantial and no question of a guarantee arises, there remains some prospect that a guarantor might be required at a future date. Indeed, some leases specifically introduce such a reference to directors in their alienation clause when contemplating a private limited company as the tenant. Although this form of clause itself is often excised, there is merit in settling in advance the form of any possible guarantee, bearing in mind the issues that have just been discussed.

4.9 Prior to leaving guarantees it is appropriate to mention the practice known as 'guarantee stripping' which may occur when a company enters into a company voluntary arrangement ('CVA') with its creditors to compromise its debts and liabilities. CVAs are increasingly popular with retailers anxious to close unprofitable stores. Detailed consideration of this insolvency procedure is outwith our scope but in essence a CVA, if approved by 75% in value of voting unsecured creditors, is binding on all subject to a court challenge to revoke on grounds of unfairness or irregularity. The concern of landlords arises where a CVA purports to discharge guarantees granted by a third party such as another company within the tenant's group, thereby stripping out such a guarantee. CVAs have exercised the (English) courts in such as the so-called Powerhouse case[1] where, although deeming that example of stripping to be unfair, the court did not find the procedure unlawful in principle. The issue has re-emerged in a recent case dubbed 'Son of Powerhouse'[2] involving Sixty UK Ltd, whose Italian parent company had guaranteed its subsidiary's obligations under two leases of units in a Liverpool shopping centre. The landlord succeeded in its application for revocation of the CVA proposed by the administrators as its effect (releasing the guarantees in exchange for

£300,000) was to deprive the landlord of recourse against the guarantor during the remainder of the leases in exchange for a sum that did not represent a fair pre-estimate of the landlord's loss. The administrators were the recipients of scathing criticism from the court for having 'abdicated their responsibilities' of acting independently. This case has thereby improved the negotiating position of landlords facing proposals for a tenant CVA, including their prospects on challenge.

---

1   *Prudential Assurance Co Ltd v PRG Powerhouse Ltd* [2007] EWHC 1890 (Ch).
2   *Mourant & Co Trustees Ltd v Sixty UK Ltd (in administration)* [2010] EWHC 1002 (Ch).

4.10 It is worth noting that there are other forms of support that may be available to a tenant whose covenant is considered too weak. These would theoretically include an insurance policy or guarantee from the tenant's bank. However the availability of either probably requires a strength of covenant which should be acceptable to the landlord without support. Of more practical importance are deposit agreements whereby an agreed sum is provided by the tenant and placed on deposit to be available for drawdown by the landlord in the event of tenant default. The Property Standardisation Group provides a style at http:/www.psglegal.co.uk. The agreement for lease, to which the draft deposit agreement should be annexed, will provide the regime for execution and registration of the deposit agreement. The following elements are worth mentioning:

- the requirement for money to be held on deposit may extend for the duration of the lease (as envisaged in the PSG style) or be limited either to a specified period or by reference to the ability of the tenant to demonstrate an appropriate covenant from the production of accounts similar to that mentioned in paragraph 4.5 in the context of a guarantor.

- for the protection of the landlord it is logical to require that at all times the sum on deposit should be no less than the equivalent of rent for an agreed period and in turn that demands that if any sums payable by the tenant, as is common, attract Value Added Tax, the deposit should include an equivalent sum (although there is no tax point at that stage) to fund a withdrawal to represent the payment and VAT thereon. Also, maintaining the full deposit requires a clause obliging the tenant to make up any shortfall within a short stated period resulting from proper withdrawals by the landlord, rent increases and VAT rises; penalty interest should run. A 'sweeper' clause referring to such as 'any other reason' may be argued by tenants to be inappropriate.

- the deposit agreement should require payment by the tenant no later than the entry date and thereafter the immediate lodging of the deposit by the landlord in an interest bearing account of a clearing bank in the name of the landlord.

- the money is stated to be held in trust, with the landlord entitled to withdraw for tenant default including the expenses of remedying any tenant breach. The PSG style allows the landlord in two circumstances to withdraw, not the sum that is due by the tenant, but the whole fund. The events are (a) the appointment of a liquidator or receiver or administrator, etc and (b) the lease being irritated. Most would argue that a return to the landlord of the whole fund is unjustified and hardly supported by the reference in the Guidance Notes to the landlord's right to 'dip into' the fund! The tenant is entitled to interest earned (usually withdrawn yearly) if the deposit level is maintained and with the responsibility to account for any tax.

- this form of regime offers to the landlord the right to withdraw money when appropriate and gives to the tenant protection against landlord insolvency. The landlord may choose to register the agreement (in Scotland or England as appropriate) where the tenant is a company.

- other provisions include those that (i) bring the irritancy provisions of the lease into play (ii) allow the return of the deposit fund to the tenant on the expiry of the deposit period or the date of a permitted assignation or renunciation or at lease termination, in which latter event containing a proviso about tenant compliance with lease obligations which can lead to delay in settlement if a terminal schedule of dilapidations is served and (iii) require the landlord (who, unlike the tenant, can assign its interest) to assign the rights and obligations under the agreement to any party acquiring the landlord's interest in the subjects of lease and transfer the whole deposit fund including interest.

THE DURATION

4.11 In leases of property not built at the date of the agreement for lease, the precise commencement and termination dates are unknown and require to be completed later by reference to the relevant provisions in the agreement (paras 2.13–2.17 and 2.31). The lease should avoid ambiguity and state calendar dates (see, for example, para 8.3).

4.12 The duration will have been fixed in negotiation. Conventionally, the length of the so-called 'institutional' lease has been 25 years but over time the market has changed. Since the 1990s, lease lengths have decreased in all sectors. Leases for 10 and 15 years are now common and are accepted by the institutional investment market. For older property not deemed of institutional quality, lease lengths have tended to be shorter and may not be subject to rent review or be reviewed at, say, three-yearly intervals.

4.13 Leaving aside the question of renewal (discussed in Chapter 11), the stated duration may be changed contractually by options to extend or break. Options to the tenant to extend contain a lack of certainty for the landlord and a requirement that the rent for the extended period be fixed, failing agreement, by a third party. The option must be exercised within the life of the original lease[1]. Options to extend are relatively rare, in contrast to break options which in recent times have enjoyed much popularity with tenants anxious to avoid unqualified commitment for too long a period in challenging economic conditions. These are considered in Chapter 11.

---

1   *Commercial Union Assurance Co Ltd and Ors* 1964 SC 84, 1964 SLT 62.

THE RENT

4.14 The rent to be paid throughout the lease must be capable of ascertainment. The agreement will provide the formula when the subjects of lease are unbuilt at the contract date (para 2.4). The initial rent will therefore be stated in the lease when executed with any review provisions enabling future rents to be ascertained. The landlord's solicitor should ensure that the tenant is required to pay the reviewed rent by 'triggering' the operation of any rent review schedule either in the letting clause or elsewhere in the lease (not the schedule). Rent is usually stated to be exclusive of value added tax, payable without deduction (save any required by law) and to be paid without demand. Two further points are worthy of mention:

- some older leases, as well as requiring interest on late payment (para 4.18), require payment 'with a fifth part more of each quarter's payment of liquidate penalty in case of failure in punctual payment'. It was held in *Council of the Borough of Wirral v Currys Group plc*[1] to be enforceable but only to the extent of any actual loss. A discussion paper on penalty clauses was issued by the Scottish Law Commission in 1997 but no subsequent action has been taken.

- the joint and several obligation mentioned in paragraph 4.3 is sometimes limited to the rent clause. In any event, the clause is effective in its terms[2] and should be revised from the tenant's perspective because it means that every tenant is a cautioner for all future rent.

---

1 *Council of the Borough or Wirral v Currys Group plc* 1997 SCLR 805.
2 *Bel Investments Pensions Fund Trustees v MacTavish* 1999 GWD 27–1294.

4.15 Rent is usually paid quarterly in advance on the quarter days at 28 February, May, August and November, with some English clients opting for their quarter days. However, across the range of tenants, both large and small, payment of rent on a monthly basis is increasingly popular. The payment date is often the first day of each month. Usually, rent starts on the date of entry, with any rent-free period being regulated in the agreement as a personal contract between developer and tenant (para 2.17). The period covered by the first instalment of rent should be stated where this is not a full rental period.

4.16 Turnover rents are considered in paragraph 8.74.

OTHER MONEY PAYMENTS

4.17 The landlord's solicitor must ensure (unless the lease is not to be fully repairing and insuring) that the landlord avoids all financial responsibility for the subjects of lease. Grouping the various recurring financial payments for which the tenant is liable together in the letting clause after rent reduces the chance of omission, particularly the failure to bring a schedule into operation. Indeed, certain of these payments are sometimes stated to be rent (which enhances the landlord's powers in England), conferring in Scotland the minor advantage of a widening of the clutches of the landlord's hypothec, which secures one year's rent over moveable items of the tenant in the subjects of lease. Few well-advised tenants accept this provision.

4.18 The financial liabilities for consideration are:

- all rates, taxes, charges etc of every kind, novel or otherwise, levied on the owner or occupier of the subjects of let. Tenants should try to exclude all taxes relating to dealings by the landlord in its interest;

- the service charge (covered elsewhere – see paras 6.30–6.39);

- the premiums on various insurance policies discussed in Chapter 7 and, as is there explained, usually placed by the landlord. The tenant may argue that the premium to be paid should be net of commission. The landlord will claim that this merely reflects a quantum discount linked to substantial property interests. In practice, most tenants do not press this point. However, tenants should be aware that if the lease is silent on the level of premiums, it is likely that the courts, in contrast to the position on service charge, would not intervene in the choice of insurer (if the criteria for selection were met) even if the premiums were substantially more than previously[1]. Where the subjects of lease are not insured separately and therefore capable of ready ascertainment there needs to be a method of apportionment among the tenants affected. Concerns such as that the nature and cost of replacement of the fitting-out works of various tenants may differ markedly, and that in industrial lets some units may have a higher fire risk, militate against an apportionment identical to service charge. Many tenants, possibly surprisingly, are inclined to accept an apportionment that is 'fair and reasonable'. Premiums on loss of rent insurance will be calculated on an individual basis;

- interest on late payments – the landlord needs a penalty interest rate (often 4 per cent above base rate) on all late payments. The tenant's solicitor should avoid this rate being applied to undetermined rent (para 8.65). Other than rent, tenants should require demands for the various payments and for interest to apply only if payment is not made within, say, 14 days of demand. Landlords should avoid words that give to the tenant a period free of interest no matter how late payment is made.

---

1   *Victor Harris (Gentswear) Ltd v Wool Warehouse (Perth)* Ltd 1995 SCLR 577; *Berrycroft Management Co Ltd and Ors v Sinclair Gardens Investments (Kensington) Ltd (and related appeals)* [1996] EGCS 143.

Chapter 5

Repairs

5.1 The purpose of an institutional lease is to make the tenant responsible for the cost of all 'repairs'. This and the next two chapters deal with the methods by which the landlord tries to maximise the scope of that liability in relation to (a) repairs by the tenant to the subjects of lease (chapter 5), (b) repairs by the landlord to all items common to the subjects of lease and other parts of a larger development but paid for by the various tenants through service charge (chapter 6) and (c) repairs whose cause is a risk against which the landlord has required insurance cover with the tenant paying the premiums (chapter 7).

5.2 The division of responsibility for the carrying out of repairs to the subjects of lease (and any common parts of the development) between landlord and tenant and the liability for the cost of such repairs is a matter upon which, at least in theory, the objective for the draftsman is to reflect the intentions of the parties as discussed and agreed in their negotiations; that drafting could cover a wide spectrum. In practice most leases (including many for which these provisions are unsuitable) are drawn initially on the basis of a fully repairing and insuring lease commonly interpreted in the context of repairs as leaving the tenant liable directly or indirectly for all repairs, no matter how fundamental or extensive. Any explanation of repairing clauses in the modern lease needs to recognise that this is the norm.

5.3 Instructions to draw repairing clauses leaving landlords free from ultimate financial responsibility originated nearly 50 years ago with the introduction of English-dominated commercial leases into our property market. Those acting for landlords, faced with the task of achieving the perceived purpose, encountered a number of obstacles in our common law.

IMPLIED LANDLORD'S WARRANTY

5.4 The first is an implied warranty by the landlord that the subjects of lease are reasonably fit for the purpose for which they are let[1]. Modern leases therefore contain an acknowledgment by the tenant that the subjects are accepted as being in good and substantial repair and in all respects suitable for the purpose for which they are let. In *Lowe v Quayle Munro Ltd*[2] the court held, after close debate, that words which required the tenant 'to accept the leased subjects in their present condition' did establish a benchmark, given the other terms of this clause, at the date of entry to which the subsequent wide obligation related. Nevertheless, it is prudent for the landlord to include an express acceptance by the tenant of the subjects and the common parts as being 'in good and substantial and tenantable repair and in all respects fit for the purpose for which they are let' (or something similar) or introduce an obligation 'to put into repair', something which is implied in England by 'to repair' (but see para 5.19 for the tenant's concerns about that phrase). Such a clause often appears in the letting clause, totally divorced from the repairing clause. The question of exclusion of and nature of that warranty is considered at length in *Mars Pension Trustees Ltd v County Properties and Developments Ltd*[3]. The case of *Blackwell*[4] made it clear that the common parts should be included specifically in this clause.

---

1   Rankine *The Law of Leases in Scotland* (3rd edn, 1916) p 240; *Paton v MacDonald* 1973 SLT (Sh Ct) 85.
2   *Lowe v Quayle Munro Ltd* 1997 SC 346.
3   *Mars Pension Trustees Ltd v County Properties and Developments Ltd* 1999 SC 267, 1999 SCLR 117.
4   *Blackwell v Farmfoods (Aberdeen) Ltd* 1991 GWD 4–219.

TENANTABLE REPAIR

5.5 The second obstacle was the common law duty on the landlord, albeit perhaps with some qualification, to keep urban subjects in tenantable repair and wind and watertight. This extends beyond ordinary repairs to include those arising due to natural decay or latent defect. To overcome this problem there must be incorporated into the lease repairing obligations sufficiently clear to impose upon the tenant all of those which, lacking the clause, would have fallen upon the landlord. Clear language must be used[1] so as to leave no doubt that the obligation has been transferred. Something along the following lines is common:

> 'At all times throughout the duration of the lease the Tenant shall at its expense well and substantially repair, renew, maintain, rebuild, reinstate, decorate and clean and generally in all respects put into and keep in good and substantial repair and condition the leased subjects and every part thereof; such obligations herein contained shall subsist irrespective of the age or state of dilapidation of the leased subjects and irrespective of the cause of the damage, deterioration or destruction whether by a defect, latent or patent which may exist at the date of entry or which may subsequently develop or from any other cause or source'.

---

1   *Turner's Trustees v Steel* (1900) 2 F 363.

5.6 It will be appreciated that the obvious feature of this common form of drafting is not the required clarity but the tautological nature of the drafting which has prompted some judicial comment. In *Lowe v Quayle Munro* Lord Penrose stated in relation to a similar clause that *'its structure is complex and its syntax challenging'* and *'the clause is anything but free from difficulty'*. Also, Lord Reed in *Westbury Estates Limited v the Royal Bank of Scotland*[1] remarked when commenting on (English) authorities that although the court should in principle give effect to each word used, in commercial leases the style of drafting may leave the court with little need or scope for finding a different shade of meaning for every word used.

---

1   *Westbury Estates Ltd Royal Bank of Scotland plc* 2006 SLT 1143.

5.7 However such a torrent of words is likely to succeed. For example, in *Thorn EMI*[1] the court was invited to decide on the width of the obligation to 'uphold, repair, maintain, renew and keep and in the event of destruction, however the same should arise, to rebuild, reinstate and replace both the exterior and interior of the premises to the satisfaction of the landlord'. The court held that because of the exclusion of any distinction in the cause of the damage it was 'apt to cover damage from an inherent defect to the building which has been present from its construction, as well as damage arising from events which took place after its erection'.

---

1   *Thorn EMI Ltd v Taylor Woodrow Industrial Estates Ltd* (29 October 1982, unreported).

5.8 The question remains whether the drafting in any particular case has enabled the landlord to transfer responsibility. Certainty is not possible as so much depends on the precise words. However, one can draw some conclusions from *Taylor Woodrow Property Co Ltd v Strathclyde Regional Council*[1]. Firstly, a phrase such as 'to the satisfaction of the landlord' is to be understood as meaning 'reasonable satisfaction'. Secondly 'repair' does not include 'extraordinary repairs' such as latent or structural defects but it may (depending on the particular drafting) include renewal of components such as a roof, if shown to be necessary.

---

1   *Taylor Woodrow Property Co Ltd v Strathclyde Regional Council* 1996 GWD 7–397.

5.9 In *Westbury Estates Limited v Royal Bank of Scotland plc* the repairing clause was in language consistent with the tenant having full responsibility including in relation to certain electrical and mechanical items which the landlord argued should be replaced, not because they were defective, but because they needed replacement in terms of guidelines on the economic life of such items laid down by the Chartered Institution of Building Services Engineers. Apart from an obvious problem that these guidelines were not in general acceptance (and may not have existed) at the date of entry, the court rejected the landlord's argument that the tenant was necessarily obliged to replace an item that had reached the end of its economic life. The fact that the item is less efficient than a more modern equivalent is unrelated to the question of whether it is in good and substantial repair and condition. This argument owes much to that stated in the *Fluor Daniel* case[1] that concerned service charge provisions (para 6.18), a case on which the tenant principally relied. In *West Castle Properties Ltd v Scottish Ministers*[2] it was held that an obligation on the tenant to keep the premises in 'the like good tenantable condition and repair' as at the start of the lease required the tenant to carry out works that a prudent owner would have carried out. The tenant was able to take account of the increasing age of the premises and had fulfilled the obligation even if the items were in a less good condition in 2007 than in 2002.

1   *Fluor Daniel Properties Ltd v Shortlands Investments Ltd* [2001] 2 EGLR 91.
2   *West Castle Properties Ltd v Scottish Ministers* 2004 SCLR 899.

REI INTERITUS

5.10 The third principle of common law which in the repairing context required consideration is the doctrine of *rei interitus* whereby the lease is brought to an end where the subjects thereof are destroyed actually or constructively from a cause outwith the control of and contemplation of the parties. The landlord would lose its income stream (anathema to a modern landlord) and the tenant would lose its occupation. This perceived fatality is overridden by a clear clause to that effect[1].

1   *Cantors Properties (Scotland) Ltd v Swears and Wells Ltd* 1978 SC 310, 1980 SLT 165.

TRANSFERENCE OF RESPONSIBILITY TO TENANT

5.11 Therefore by careful drafting extending often over several clauses, the common law principles whose effect was a sharing of responsibility for repairs between landlord and tenant can be overcome so as to shift total responsibility to the tenant. But in trying to achieve such a state of affairs the landlord's solicitor must consider carefully the structure of the lease. We have considered elsewhere (paras 3.1–3.4) the extent of the property and in this context the landlord should ensure clarity on the definition of the subjects of lease, including fixtures (para 3.5). Where the landlord owns all of the property it is leasing it would usually choose to lease that property to include structure, probably by reference to a property title. Where (as in a tenement or in an estate with privately maintained common access roads) there would be common repair costs to be borne in mind, these would usually be treated by requiring the tenant to pay them to the relief of the landlord although it should be noted that, irrespective of the words used, there may be practical problems in requiring a tenant to effect reconstruction (or some similar word) of premises which form part of a tenement[1]. The option of requiring the tenant to carry out with others common repairs in terms of the property title makes little sense in multi-occupancy buildings such as office blocks or modern shopping centres. The demands of such sophisticated structures with common areas such as pedestrian malls, circulation areas, atria, plant and equipment require considerable management. Landlords will wish to avoid practical problems of getting a number of tenants to agree where important repairs may be necessary to common parts. In the context of repair, therefore, where the subjects of lease exclude all structural elements, the importance is transferred from the direct repairing clause to service expenditure and service charge provisions which are considered in Chapter 6.

1   *Flockhart v GA Properties Ltd* 2001 GWD 37–1410.

5.12 Despite the drafting techniques used to ensure that the whole responsibility of direct repairs falls upon the tenant, both parties to the lease should bear in mind that, both from a legal point of view in a consideration of the common law obligations and from a practical standpoint directed towards preservation of the landlord's investment, any limitation in the transference of obligations to the tenant automatically leaves such obligations with the landlord. An example can be found in the case of *House of Fraser plc v Prudential Assurance Co Ltd*[1]. A clause in the lease bound the landlord to keep in good and substantial repair the foundations, roof, main walls and main structural members, with a further clause requiring the tenant to reimburse the landlord the cost of such repairs. The landlord proposed to rebuild a retaining wall in urgent need of repair. The tenant argued that this was an extraordinary repair, for which the landlord had responsibility at common law, for which there was no corresponding provision in the lease and accordingly, reimbursement did not arise. It was held that the terms of the lease were sufficiently wide to include ordinary and extraordinary repairs and that even if the repair was an extraordinary repair the landlord had responsibility under the lease and the tenant was obliged to reimburse the cost. The importance of this case is that, because a landlord has at common law an obligation for extraordinary repairs, a relatively simple restatement of that obligation combined with a reimbursement clause is sufficient to leave the tenant exposed. However, had this been a direct repairing clause it is considered unlikely that, lacking clarity of drafting, the tenant would have been found liable because the common law obligation cannot be displaced easily. It follows also that, if the various obstacles are overcome, such as to leave the tenant with total responsibility, an exclusion specifically so drafted has to be considered with care. The common exclusion of damage by the insured risks will afford to the tenant only such relief as the precise drafting will allow.

1   *House of Fraser plc v Prudential Assurance Co Ltd* 1994 SLT 416.

5.13 The wholesale transference of liability from landlord to tenant could produce inequitable results, no more so than in circumstances where major rebuilding would be required from such as an inherent defect with very little time remaining in the lease and (unlike England) no security of tenure, save that limited security afforded by the Tenancy of Shops (Scotland) Act 1964. It is, therefore, all the more ironic that in England the law has not and does not leave the tenant with such a broad area of responsibility. It is true that the word 'repair' has in England always meant more than strict repair[1] and that the repairing obligation does extend to latent defect and to the work to remedy that defect[2] but in England there is no doctrine of inherent defect. The question is one of degree, not causation, and cases turn on their own circumstances. In general terms the tenant is not there obliged to remedy a defect (inherent or otherwise) which would amount to a reconstruction of substantially the whole of the subjects or giving back to the landlord something wholly different from that leased. There is, therefore, in England some limitation on the liability of the tenant.

1   *Lurcott v Wakely and Wheeler* [1911] 1 KB 905.
2   *Ravenseft Properties Ltd v Davstone (Holdings) Ltd* [1980] 1 QB 12.

5.14 However, in Scotland leases written in language consistent with the success of transference of total liability to the tenant have been written for decades for good-quality property, such that the investment market in Scotland has existed on the back of such leases. The effect is to reduce in value those properties leased on terms less advantageous to the landlord, albeit that the rent might be increased (see para 8.43 at (ii)). Whatever the equity, the objective of the landlord is a lease which has no deduction from landlord's income for any liability to repairs and such as will enhance the value of the investment thereby created. This then has represented the norm, however disadvantageous it may seem from the viewpoint of tenants. It is entirely legitimate to mount a defence for such leases, certainly where major investment by the landlord is required, where the building leased has been erected since such leases became commonplace and where the duration is relatively long. The further one moves from that position, the more difficult it becomes to justify the landlord's stance. Where a long, complex draft lease is submitted incorporating a full rebuilding obligation, including latent defects, in circumstances in which the property is old, where the area is perhaps known to have subsidence difficulties, where the property is a small ground-floor shop in an elderly tenement and where the duration is limited, that lease becomes very difficult to defend. The pity is that many tenants seem prepared, whether knowingly or otherwise, to accept such provisions. The solicitor acting for the tenant should bear all of this in mind when faced with the documentation and should have regard to risk evaluation. Major commercial tenants with the required resources, however unwillingly, are often prepared to accept full rebuilding obligations on the analysis that the discovery of a major structural problem in one unit out of many is an acceptable risk. But if the tenant is an individual or a small partnership, perhaps with only one property, the result of that experience could be personal bankruptcy and, ironically, such a tenant is statistically more likely to take the short-term lease of the ground-floor shop with potential for the roof being 'nail sick' and where the apportionment of common repairs could be according to rateable value or on some other method unhelpful to the commercial property in the block.

COMMON TENANT'S REVISALS

5.15 Against that background, which may include difficult prevailing market conditions, the tenant's solicitor requires to consider carefully his approach to a direct repairing clause (for service charge implications, see paras 6.14–6.19) imposing on his/her client a full rebuilding obligation. However, in that consideration, the client's knowledge of the likely condition of the subjects of lease (including any larger property of which they form part) is central. Advice on a proper survey (including that of landlords' fixtures and fittings such as items of plant and machinery) is no different from that applicable to a purchase although it is recognised that there are limitations where the property is not built (see para 2.19) or is part of a very large development. Among the possible revisals to the repairing clause which a tenant may try, depending upon circumstances, are the following:

5.16 Because most leases place upon the landlord an obligation (at the expense of the tenants of the development) to insure against certain identified risks and to use the policy proceeds in restoring damage, landlords offer no objection to insured risk damage being excluded from the tenant's liability, save to the extent that money is irrecoverable due to the act or default of the tenant. For such an exclusion to be effective, care needs to be taken in framing the insurance provisions in matters such as the spread of risks, avoiding subrogation rights, excess provisions and related matters, including provisions for such as acts of terrorism and the drafting consequences. If the landlord agrees to accept responsibility for certain risks against which insurance cover may not be available (often called 'Uninsured Risks'), this should be specifically excluded from the direct repairing clause (see para 6.15 for the similar point relative to service expenditure). The subject of uninsured risks is considered in Chapter 7.

5.17 In limited circumstances, often in leases of short duration, and in reality only if the principle has been established during negotiations, parties may agree that the tenant's liability be limited to 'internal repairs', with the landlord being bound at its expense to carry out all other repairs. Tenants' solicitors so instructed should ensure that 'internal' comprises only plasterwork and decorative finishes and indeed any negotiations which conclude with a sharing of responsibility should prompt careful consideration of definitions such as 'structural' to ensure that no gap is left for which nobody has responsibility.

5.18 Where the subjects of lease comprise part or the whole of an older property, particular care is required from the tenant's angle. The chances of a major repair arising may be higher than in a newer property and there will be no collateral warranties available (see paras 2.27–2.28). The results of a structural survey should inform the attitude of the tenant. Although landlords will universally argue for a usual full rebuilding clause, parties may agree that the obligations of the tenant be limited to maintaining the subjects of lease in at least as good a condition as is evidenced by a schedule of condition. An increased use of schedules of condition may reflect the property market downturn. Those preparing the schedule should be advised to provide an accurate statement of condition (often supported by photographs) to avoid disputes on interpretation and the tenant would need to be assured that it was practical for the building to be occupied without the need for fundamental repairs. An alternative is to qualify the obligations of the tenant by terms such as 'fair, wear and tear excepted' but substantial difficulties of interpretation could arise and in consequence this option is relatively uncommon.

5.19 Where, as is normal, the circumstances are not present for repairs to be limited either to those of an internal nature or by reference to a schedule of condition, revisals for the tenant beyond excluding insured risk damage (para 5.16) are likely to be focussed on avoiding liability for:

- making good items of repair that are known to exist at the date of entry; if these repairs are not to be undertaken immediately at the landlord's cost (the preferred option), the tenant's solicitor should excise words such as 'put into' which would have that effect;

- latent or inherent defect, generally considered to mean a defect found to be existing but not visible at the date of entry caused by a defect in design, materials, workmanship or supervision during the construction process. As discussed, the type of repairing clause conventionally employed by landlords would include latent defect: indeed the clause set forth in paragraph 5.5 does so in three separate ways, namely by the use of both 'put into' and, 'irrespective of the cause' and also by a specific reference. To exclude liability for latent defect (even for an initial period of, say, five years) remains a difficult task for the tenant in good-quality property. If such an exclusion is agreed, a definition of the term and the parts of the building to which it applies should be introduced. Latent defect insurance policies are becoming somewhat more common and similar care will be required in writing the policy. This subject is considered in paragraph 2.21;

- any renewal, replacement or rebuilding of elements that are not beyond economic repair. For the tenant to wish, if practicable, to repair an element rather than be required to undertake a more expensive option is understandable and such a clarifying revisal is commonly acceptable to landlords;

- any repairing obligations to the extent that the work (eg major rebuilding) requires the permission of some competent authority, which permission is unavailable despite all reasonable endeavours by the tenant. This is not dissimilar from the protection required by the landlord in respect of insured risk damage (para 7.14). Nevertheless, such a revisal is likely to provoke resistance from the landlord, concerned at a possible dilution of fundamental obligations of the tenant.

5.20 Two general points are worthy of mention here. Firstly, one should in tackling direct repairing clauses bear in mind the extent to which the subjects of lease may exclude structural elements. If so, it is not a forensic triumph for the tenant to exclude liability for such as latent defect in non-structural items unless the equivalent exclusion appears in the service charge provisions (para 6.16). Secondly, concessions on repairing liability are sometimes offered by the landlord in a back letter. There are dangers for the tenant in that arrangement which are considered in paragraphs 2.32–2.36.

DILAPIDATIONS

5.21 Having fixed the extent of the repairing obligations of the tenant, the landlord's solicitor must ensure that the lease includes a regime that secures compliance by the tenant with those principal repairing responsibilities, and any other duties of the tenant bearing upon the physical condition of the subjects of lease. These would include alterations and signage (paras 9.39–9.46), compliance with statute and title (paras 9.48–9.53), and decoration (para 9.54). With a view to the exercise of one or more of the remedies identified in paragraph 5.23 in the event of a breach by the tenant, the landlord's solicitor would be expected to include in the lease a clause (or clauses):

- obliging the tenant within an appropriate timescale to give to the landlord relevant information about the condition of the subjects of lease. This would include any damage suffered (and to the extent caused by an insured risk), any major defects or any repairs notice;

- giving the landlord (and agents) access for inspection and for the service of an interim schedule of dilapidations. Unless the lease imposes a restriction, the landlord can repeat the exercise as often as it wants. The special issues surrounding terminal schedules of dilapidations are discussed in paragraphs 11.25–11.27;

- requiring the tenant to be responsible for all costs incurred by the landlord for inspections, preparation of schedules of dilapidations and monitoring of works. The tenant is likely to wish such costs to be 'reasonable' or, failing that, 'reasonably and properly' incurred;

- identifying the address to which formal notices, including schedules of dilapidations, are to be sent and any other procedural requirements. Most tenants resist service being to the subjects of lease, unless also sent to their registered office, if a company (para 2.47);

- allowing the tenant a period (often six weeks) to complete the repair works to the landlord's (reasonable) satisfaction. Where the work is not minor, that period (part of which will be taken up with placing the contract) is too short. Tenants usually agree to a material start within that period and an obligation to complete the works with all reasonable speed. However, landlords should avoid being too generous as major defects should be remedied by the tenant without the compulsitor of a schedule;

- allowing the landlord the right (which is not available at common law as it derogates from the grant of exclusive possession), failing action by the tenant, to enter the subjects of lease and carry out the work at the cost of the tenant, including professional fees and penalty interest to the date of reimbursement. The extent of such a reservation requires to be considered carefully (para 3.15).

5.22 Despite well-drawn provisions in the lease, dilapidations provide fertile ground for disputes. The tenant, facing unwelcome expense, may be aggrieved at a schedule requiring an unreasonably high standard of repair or including items of doubtful relevance. That sense of grievance on the part of the tenant may be increased if the schedule is served during negotiations for rent review or the consideration of a request for consent to assign, leading to the suspicion that the timing may be tactical. Conversely, the landlord may resent needing to spend time and trouble enforcing a fundamental obligation of the tenant where none of the available remedies is ideal. Although there is no specific form of schedule of dilapidations it will serve to reduce the prospects of dispute, including about fee levels, if the landlord and any building surveyor employed for the purpose, by checking the lease and any ancillary documents eg a back letter, ensure that, firstly, all of the work demanded is the proper and direct responsibility of the tenant and secondly, the schedule is served in accordance with any procedural requirements of the lease.

5.23 The remedies available to the landlord during the lease are:

- an application to the court for a decree of specific implement following failure by the tenant to comply with a schedule of dilapidations. Provided that the obligation is clear, a court is likely to grant the remedy unless satisfied in all the circumstances that it would not be fair and reasonable. This remedy is unlikely to be attractive to a landlord who considers that this work needs immediate attention, nor is it competent after the lease expiry date[1]. It should be noted that a similar remedy of specific performance in England is generally thought to be unavailable during the lease;

- the landlord may do the work and recover the cost. For this remedy to be available, the lease needs to contain the clause referred to in paragraph 5.21 (bullet point 6) authorising the exercise of such a right. The problem here is that the landlord must spend the money and then try to recover the cost plus interest and expenses and there is often room for debate about the precise extent of the works required;

- on failure by the tenant, and where the landlord can prove loss, an action for damages. This is a remedy which has greater relevance at the end of a lease, this being discussed in paragraph 11.27. However one could envisage a landlord seeking damages where the failure of the tenant could be shown to have prejudiced either a sale of the landlord's interest or the raising of funds secured over it;

- an action of irritancy is discussed in paragraphs 11.6–11.15. The essential question is whether the so-called 'fair and reasonable' landlord would seek irritancy where there are other remedies available. In *Euro Properties Ltd v Alam and Mitchell*[2] the court held that a fair and reasonable landlord in the position of the pursuer would not try to irritate the lease having regard to the available alternative remedies. In the words of Lord Macfadyen '...it is not *prima facie* fair and reasonable to opt for irritancy where there is available an alternative remedy...which would (a) not deprive the tenant of his interest in the lease but (b) nevertheless protect the landlord' interests'. Other factors for consideration where the action, if successful, would allow the tenant to escape from the lease are the covenant strength of the tenant and prevailing market conditions.

---

1   *PIK Facilities Ltd v Shell UK Ltd* 2003 SLT 155.
2   *Euro Properties Ltd v Alam and Mitchell* 2000 GWD 23–896.

5.24 The remedies available to the tenant for failure by a landlord to comply with its obligations of repair, express or implied, are:

- an action of specific implement such as has been described in paragraph 5.23 in the context of a failure by the tenant.

- following the failure of the landlord to comply within a reasonable timescale with a notice from the tenant identifying the wants of repair, the tenant can pursue a claim for damages assessed in the normal manner that applies to a breach of contract.

- a remedy that may, arguably, produce a quicker resolution for the tenant is that of doing the required work and setting this off against future rent payments. Such a right exists at common law. In practice this will rarely be the selected course of action as most leases contain prohibitions against set-off and in any event, the tenant may fear consequent irritancy procedure.

- in the event that the landlord is in fundamental material breach of the lease, the tenant has the remedy of termination by rescission (para 11.29) but in practice this option does not appear to commend itself to tenants.

5.25 The remedies of the parties at termination of the lease have, in the case of the landlord, narrowed from the four items identified in paragraph 5.23 to two and in the case of the tenant have for all practical purposes disappeared. These are discussed in the context of termination issues generally, including reinstatement of alterations by the tenant, in paragraph 11.27.

5.26 Finally on repairs, the landlord may consider that managing agents' fees should be the responsibility of the tenant. Where there are service charge provisions (Chapter 6), that is inevitable although the tenant needs to consider limiting them. However a tenant in occupation of the whole building for which it has a direct repairing responsibility will be reluctant to pay for someone merely to inspect the subjects of lease on the basis that, if any schedule is found to be justified, the consequential costs would be recovered by the landlord. Further, such provisions often disguise the right of the landlord to recover fees paid for more regular advice and valuations provided by managing agents as part of their 'comprehensive' service to clients.

Chapter 6

Service Charge

INTRODUCTION

6.1 In Chapter 5 we saw that where the subjects of lease are not part of a larger property belonging to the landlord, the structure is leased to the tenant who thereby has direct responsibility for all repairs. This usually applies even if an item such as a common access road is used, with the tenant taken bound to reimburse the landlord a proportion of costs incurred by the landlord; the tenant should in these cases ensure that the landlord is bound to carry out the work or require performance from a third party.

6.2 In both of the other situations considered in Chapter 5, where the subjects of lease exclude structural elements or where, as in a retail park for example, there are highly important common items such as car parking areas, the lease should contain detailed service charge provisions.

6.3 In modern developments, service costs can be considerable, particularly in enclosed shopping centres, and it is important for a prospective tenant to obtain early information about the likely liability. For existing developments, previous accounts should be examined, possibly coupled with inquiries about anticipated future expenditure on major items. For new developments, tenants should demand estimates and try, where possible, to negotiate a 'cap' for an initial period.

6.4 Lastly by way of introduction, the objective of the landlord is to ensure that the total cost of providing any services which it chooses to perform is borne by the tenants. Careful drafting is required and advice should be taken from the prospective managing agents (in-house or external) who will put these provisions into practice. There are broadly three strands within what are called generically the service charge provisions, namely:

(i)   the range of services;

(ii)   the cost of providing them (the service expenditure);

(iii) the liability of the tenant, including the mechanics of recovery (the service charge).

Although these strands are frequently interwoven in drafting techniques, it aids understanding to consider them separately. Prior to that exercise it is appropriate to make reference to a new important code of practice on service charges.

THE RICS CODE OF PRACTICE ('THE CODE')

6.5 Given the importance and sophistication of service charge provisions particularly in major developments, it is no surprise that their negotiation and subsequent operation have rarely been without controversy and dispute. Recognising this, on 11 September 2007 the RICS introduced the Scottish Edition of a code of practice applying to service charges commencing on or after 1 April 2008, intended to embody 'best practice'. The Code has the status of a guidance note to its members. A new version of the Code, covering the whole of the UK, is to take effect from 1 October 2011.

6.6 Although in any particular case it is the lease that will set out the contractual position, the recommendation is that new leases will be 'aligned with the Code'. Existing leases with provisions inconsistent with the Code are to be 'interpreted so far as possible with the principles and practices {of the Code} unless the lease specifically stipulates a different approach'. The aim of ensuring that, by the application of the Code, leases will generally contain a fair and balanced service charge regime is not entirely without practical difficulty even with general acceptance of the Code by the property industry. It will take time for existing leases with non-compliant provisions to expire and those in a development that do so (whether at their natural expiry or earlier termination) and are replaced by new compliant ones may result in dual service charge and consequent rental implications. At least in Scotland, when the natural expiry date is reached, the terms of any agreed new lease are generally not constrained by a statutory right of lease renewal (paragraph 11.24).

6.7 The discussion in this chapter of the three general strands of service charge provisions identified in paragraph 6.4 will consider the usual negotiating issues and then the recommendations of the Code. It should be borne in mind that the Code is intended to be a 'package' that is fair between parties, recognising that managers owe a duty of care to tenants who are paying for the services and to owners whose investment needs proper management. Meetings at which parties evince confidence in the Code yet indulge in the 'cherry-picking' of elements that suit their purpose will not bring any improvement to the pre-Code position.

THE SERVICES

6.8 The landlord wants the range of services to encompass anything which it considers necessary to maintain the development in good condition capable of competing in a changing environment. This demand is fulfilled by the solicitor drafting a comprehensive list and a 'sweeper' clause. The nature of the list is governed by the type and sophistication of the development and its physical features and can vary widely. However, in general, 'services' will comprise those which:

(i)   are aimed at maintaining the physical condition of the development (by which is meant the whole structure less parts let to tenants), including all plant and machinery and unbuilt-on areas like car parks, service roads etc;

(ii)   consist of payments to be made by the landlord, such as for rates, gas and electricity, refuse collection etc;

(iii)   relate to security, operating car parks etc, including staff costs and facilities;

(iv)   are payments to professional staff and consultants, eg managing agents, insurance valuers, accountants and other advisers including lawyers;

(v)   in the case of retail centres are initiatives designed to promote the centre.

6.9 Having established with the landlord and the managing agents the list of required services to suit the development, the solicitor must include a sweeper clause to avoid tenants denying liability for an unlisted service from which they are deriving an obvious necessary benefit. Any tenant will wish to restrict such unidentified services to those from which it and the other tenants generally are obtaining advantages and which are in accordance with the principles of good estate management. It is possible that this general reference to good estate management which tends to appear in a variety of places in service charge clauses will be supplanted or enlarged by a reference to the principles of the Code.

6.10 The distinction between the ambit of the services and tenant liability therefor is not always understood. The tenant's interests are not best served by its solicitor automatically eliminating services, ostensibly to reduce cost. For example, a tenant intent on avoiding any responsibility for latent defect damage should not dilute the nature or standard of 'service' to be provided by the landlord but should exclude the cost from service expenditure. However, in considering the list of services, the tenant's solicitor would do well to focus on these matters:

(i)   many leases, as originally drafted, lack any obligation on the landlord to provide any of the services, being confined to a right to recover costs if the landlord performs or intends to do so. But services such as maintaining the structure, security or cleaning, or doing any work required by statute to allow the development to remain open or occupied, are essential. The tenant's solicitor must structure the draft to include an obligation upon the landlord to perform these core services and a discretion as to the provision of the remainder. This leads to concerns from the landlord about guaranteeing performance, including issues as to standard which will be considered in paragraph 6.13;

(ii)   although, as mentioned, tenants should be slow to dilute the services and instead should concentrate on limiting exposure to service expenditure, the list of 'services' will include those which are more expressions of liability for some kind of cost or charge rather than anything that requires positive performance from the landlord. The tenant's solicitor can 'cap' or eliminate any such charge either in the list of services or in the major revisal qualifying service expenditure (paras 6.14–6.23);

(iii)   a common example of eliminating a 'service' from the list is in relation to a sinking fund. This is a term used to describe a procedure whereby the landlord requires payment from tenants with (and additional to) each payment of service charge of sums intended to build up a fund available to finance infrequent major items of expenditure on the structure or on plant and equipment. Sinking funds are not to be confused with reserve funds built up to equalise expenditure on regularly recurring (but infrequent) service items like decoration. The advantage to the landlord of the availability of funds for items of major expenditure is obvious but on the introduction of such clauses many tenants, including major space users, were highly resistant. They demanded a raft of protections, including that:

- the anticipated expenditure be properly calculated with reference to identified items of likely expenditure and subject to a final decision of an expert or arbiter;

- all expenditure must be anticipated to arise during the currency of the lease;

- all sums collected be placed in a trust fund bearing a competitive rate of interest and separate from the landlord's assets, unaffected by the sale of the landlord's interest and thereby not within the clutches of any liquidator of the landlord;

- when expenditure is needed on an identified item, the landlord uses the sinking fund and cannot inflate normal service charge;

- the responsibility for all un-let units lies with the landlord (para 6.36);

- a recognition that the fund comprises money contributed by the tenants who are entitled to professional accountancy practices which mitigate tax liabilities, identify the extent of these accrued payments for any purpose (including assignation) and provide for the return of unused funds at the natural termination of the lease.

6.11 More fundamentally, major tenants whose ability to pay for expensive items of expenditure when they occur is not subject to serious question are unenthusiastic about a landlord requiring them to lock away funds in a trustee investment yielding a minimal return and over which they have no control. A combination of resistance from tenants and increasing taxation complications for landlords have combined to result in both sinking and reserve funds being rare in practice, certainly in leases being granted in recent times. Even where the lease contains the necessary provisions such funds are rarely established. In times when all tenants are actively looking for ways to improve cash flow, including reduction of advance rent payment periods, and when lease durations are shortening it seems unlikely that sinking and reserve funds will enjoy any new popularity with tenants. However, the Code surprisingly concludes that, subject to the type of protections just listed, it 'may make sense' to spread the cost of major expenditure.

SERVICE EXPENDITURE

6.12 At its simplest, service expenditure is the total annual cost incurred by the landlord in providing the agreed range of services. There are three matters for consideration, namely:

(i) value for money (para 6.13);

(ii) excluding costs which the tenant considers the landlord should bear (paras 6.14–6.23);

(iii) adding any sources of income which should reduce that expenditure (paras 6.24–6.29).

6.13 Landlords are understandably nervous about the prospects of endless disputes with individual tenants about the standard of performance of the services and the cost thereof and leases are drafted to allow them considerable discretion. Efforts to include words like 'with due efficiency and economy' or even 'reasonable standard' are often resisted as is the introduction of expert determination. But unless the lease stipulates otherwise, a landlord is unlikely to be able to recover fully if the work done is excessively costly or carried out to a totally unjustified standard[1]. Landlords also wish (and this extends beyond service charge) to exclude liability for any acts or negligence of their employees or contractors, a matter upon which the tenant should offer resistance, arguing that no such advantage is conferred upon the tenant and that the Unfair Contract Terms Act 1977 may apply. Tenants should, however, recognise that it is not in the interests of the landlord to provide poor value for money because the 'tone' of the development and the level of service charge in comparison with the competition will be reflected in rental levels at review. In turn, landlords should ensure proper and timely consultation with their tenants in the interests of transparency, whatever the precise obligations in the lease. The Code has much to say on the need for contractors and services suppliers to match written performance standards, with the aim of achieving value for money and effective service, rather than necessarily the lowest price.

---

1   *Lowe v Quayle Munro Ltd* 1997 SC 346.

6.14 The costs which a tenant may argue should be excluded vary with the services but are most readily illustrated by examples relevant to an enclosed shopping centre. The service expenditure would be stated to exclude, with the intent that the same be the responsibility of the landlord, the costs of the following:

6.15 restoring insured risk damage and damage caused by any of the 'Uninsured Risks' if relevant (para 7.10). The reasons for and drafting of this exclusion are similar to those that are discussed with reference to the direct repairing clause in paragraph 5.16;

6.16 repairing latent defect damage. This was discussed at paragraph 5.19 and for the reasons there mentioned is commonly resisted by the landlord in leases of usual length and of good-quality property; Furthermore, the exclusion is much more significant in service charge than in the direct repairing clause in cases where major structural elements et cetera are retained by the landlord;

6.17 the initial design and construction of the development including the equipping and fitting out. Most landlords recognise the legitimacy of this exclusion but problems arise regarding the 'provision' of items such as public facilities particularly if the installation of things like CCTV would reduce security costs. A common compromise is to exclude such items if provided within, say, three years of practical completion, thereby avoiding tenants paying for elements which should have been part of the original development;

6.18 the replacement of an item of plant and equipment with an improved system or item or the introduction of a wholly new item unless it can be justified on a financial basis. The Code endorses that view, pointing to the common sense of allowing improvements and enhancements if this is sound business sense. Support for this is found in the *Fluor Daniel* case[1]. This considered a conventional service charge clause requiring the various tenants to pay for expenditure incurred by the landlord in meeting its repairing obligations. The landlord claimed the cost of removing and replacing air conditioning plant and although the judge accepted that in principle the landlord could decide how to discharge its obligations it was not reasonable to replace an item of plant at the expense of the tenants just because it had reached the end of its recommended lifespan. Rather it was necessary to show that the plant was suffering from a defect making repair, amendment or renewal necessary and the standard of repair should not exceed that for which the tenants could be reasonably expected to pay having regard to the unexpired residue of the lease;

---

1   *Fluor Daniel Properties Ltd v Shortlands Investments Ltd* [2001] 2 EGLR 91.

6.19 any improvements above usual maintenance and repair, including rebuilding where necessary for proper repair. This is a difficult area for both parties. At one extreme, tenants should not pay for major refurbishment works, often timed to coincide with rent reviews, resulting in tenants paying increased rents due to their own expenditure. Against that, a planned refurbishment may have caused deferred costs on repairs and the newly improved and efficient environment may reduce service expenditure in the long term and bring trading benefits. One could argue that a sensible approach by the landlord to the costs of any major refurbishment is likely to be productive given the inevitable disruption to tenants whose co-operation will be important. The Code appears to take the view that the cost of any refurbishment or redevelopment (as opposed to the cost of any deferred repair costs included therewith), will be excluded from service charge;

6.20 matters between the landlords and the other tenants such as promoting the development to potential tenants, lettings, collection of rents, consents for alteration, rent reviews etc; this is unlikely to cause difficulty;

6.21 those that should in equity be borne by unusual lettings such as a food court or a car park if commercially operated;

6.22 unless handled in the list of services (para 6.10 (ii)) all costs such as fees to managing agents should be 'capped' and/or restricted to work properly and necessarily done in providing the services. Similarly, all staff costs should be suitably qualified. On these matters, landlords and their advisers are likely to be cautious;

6.23 all 'promotions' aimed at potential customers. These can cover a wide range but national tenants with substantial advertising budgets are disinclined to allow property owners to spend their money on such activities as television campaigns over which they have no control. The funding of promotional activities should, it is submitted, be regarded as a shared cost (a 50% contribution by the landlord is regularly agreed) and any proposals should be carefully discussed with tenants. This element frequently causes the parties difficulties in reaching agreement.

6.24 Many developments generate income, (often called 'mall income') usually from common areas which are maintained at the expense of the tenants. Landlords wish to maximise income but any solicitor acting for a tenant should consider requiring that the income from the following be credited to the service expenditure account, in each case under deduction of reasonable and proper expenses:

6.25 promotions and displays in the common parts such as the shopping mall. Landlords should resist this if applied to kiosks or barrows, particularly if such items pay any contribution to service expenditure;

6.26 car parks if not commercially let or contributing fairly by way of service charge;

6.27 public telephones, toilet vending machines, photocopiers etc if the cost of providing these items has been borne by the tenants through service charge;

6.28 those sums, if any (net of all costs), which the landlord recovers from the building contractors and the professional team employed by the landlord or its predecessors to construct the development, the landlord being required to use all reasonable endeavours to recover; landlords generally accept this;

6.29 all sums receivable from neighbouring proprietors for maintenance of any items common to such properties and the development; landlords would refer 'received'.

SERVICE CHARGE

6.30 This is the proportion of service expenditure charged to an individual tenant. Expressing service charge as a form of rent is not recommended (para 4.17). Because the landlord will have settled the basic format, including the method of apportionment, with the anchor tenant the room for manoeuvre of subsequent tenants is limited. As mentioned in paragraph 6.31 (bullet point 3) the landlord must avoid difficulty with subsequent lettings prompted by a format already agreed with a major tenant which is less than fair to the prospective tenants. The following two elements need consideration:

    (i)   apportionment;
    (ii)   mechanics of recovery.

Apportionment

6.31 Parties would generally accept that the basis of apportionment to each tenant should be fair and reasonable having regard to the size of units, the uses and the benefits derived and that (although some leases provide otherwise) the landlord should bear any shares applicable to un-let units. The common bases are:

- a fixed percentage (or amount). This is clear and simple but offers no flexibility even if the size of the development alters;

- rateable value. The proportion payable by a tenant is the percentage that the rateable value of the subjects of lease bears to the total rateable value of the development with provision for recalculation as rateable values alter. However some tenants may successfully appeal their rateable value (so that tenants of identical units would pay a different proportion), a successful appellant could demand repayment of sums overpaid and the whole system may be reformed. Very few leases currently granted would contain this method;

- floor area. This is by far the most common, usually by reference to the then current Code of Measuring Practice of the RICS which has the effect of reducing the prospects of disputes. It sets out definitions relating to the measurement of buildings. Usually, gross internal area is applied to warehouses and industrial buildings with net internal area being used for offices and shops. In large shopping centres a formula is usually devised to apply a weighted floor area to reflect the different costs in servicing units of differing size. By this method the larger space users pay somewhat less and accommodation on less favoured levels, such as basement, is treated similarly. Also, the anchor tenant may be able to negotiate special reductions. All prospective tenants should ask for an apportionment schedule to ensure that a weighted floor area basis has been fairly produced. If it transpires that the leases to any other tenants have been weighted so heavily as to amount to a concession by the landlord, it would be reasonable for the landlord to bear that concession as for the shares of any un-let units.

6.32 These other points are worthy of mention:

(i) In mixed-use buildings (such as ground-floor retail with offices above or a shopping centre with leisure components such as a multiplex cinema) occupiers will enjoy the services to different extents and possibly at different times of the day, the most obvious being lifts. In such situations the service expenditure may have to be divided into separate parts and apportioned according to classes of use.

(ii)   Landlords may wish, after fixing the basis according to floor area, weighted or otherwise, to reserve the right to make alterations if changes to the size of the development or the levels of use of particular tenants or other changes of circumstances so require. Tenants would wish to require that any such alteration should be fair and equitable to all tenants involved.

(iii)   The Code is generally consistent with the above.

Mechanics of Recovery

6.33 The landlord's solicitor in discussion with any managing agent must provide a proper mechanism whereby all of the tenants reimburse their due proportion of the service expenditure. Where the landlord has elected to waive exemption from VAT, it will be charged at the appropriate rate on all service charge payments invoiced to the tenant as vouched by a VAT invoice. Where the landlord is only partially exempt the tenant may not be able to effect full recovery. Except where the development or building is small and little expenditure is envisaged, payments will be on the basis of quarterly estimates, reconciled annually with expenditure incurred. The following matters require consideration by the parties.

6.34 The details of the fixing of the service year, any changes in that procedure and the timing of the production of estimates, budgets and reconciliations do not usually create difficulty. Tenants must recognise that a regime already in place in earlier deals should not be changed unless fundamentally flawed. However, a tenant can legitimately argue that the landlord (and its managing agents) should be required to adhere to reasonable timescales in the interests of proper administration.

6.35 The estimate of likely service expenditure should be provided prior to the relevant service year. The Code suggests at least one month before. Landlords dislike any constraints on their discretion to fix these estimates but usually accept terms such as 'fair and reasonable'. Tenants concerned at the prospect of deliberately inflated figures may take comfort from the next paragraph.

6.36 Service charge provisions exist to allow the landlord proper management control of an investment and to recoup the proper expenses from the tenants. They do not exist to provide for the landlord any profit on the exercise, even by way of cash flow advantages. As the Code states, service charge should be on a 'not for profit, not for loss' basis. This is not intended to prevent managers or suppliers of services from making a profit, but recognises that transparency and fairness are required. Accordingly, all sums received from tenants need to be placed into a service charge account bearing a proper return and supported by good accountancy practices open to external audit procedures. Tenants may reasonably expect that all payments of service charge, including any due by the landlord for un-let units, are credited timeously to the account and that any late payers are charged interest, itself to be so credited. With such a regime there is no compelling reason for any landlord to inflate estimates.

6.37 The landlord should be required to submit certified accounts within, say, six months of the service year end, prepared in a format which identifies heads of expenditure and their relevant breakdown. Although one would not expect such detail to appear in the lease, good practice suggests a level of detail that enables the tenants to understand clearly the costs incurred, including on-site management expenses, the results of any tendering exercise, variances from previous years and the sums credited by way of income. The Code provides a detailed list of the components of the minimum information to be provided. A reasonable period should be allowed for enquiries.

6.38 When the reconciliation procedure is completed, the landlord usually provides that shortfalls are due immediately but overpayments are credited against future quarterly payments unless the lease is due to expire. Tenants sometimes require immediate repayment with interest where the overpayment exceeds an agreed figure.

6.39 Partial damage to a development may result in a particular unit requiring to close even although much of the rest of the development remains open and thereby continues to generate service expenditure. Parties would be wise to consider insuring against loss of service charge and to abate it, just as for rent.

GREEN ISSUES

6.40 The extent to which the service charge provisions reflect green issues is, as with the range of services referred to in paragraphs 6.8–6.11, dependant on the nature of the development and the objectives of the parties. However in a sophisticated multi-occupancy development, the services will be expected to include complying with the environmental legislation affecting the development except to the extent that this is the responsibility of any tenant (paras 9.52 and 9.53) and including a green management plan, regular assessment of the energy performance of the development, the provision of separate metering of energy and water consumption of each tenant, obtaining or displaying an EPC, inspection of air conditioning systems and providing advice to tenants on reducing energy consumption. The services could be expanded to require the provision of dedicated recycling facilities and appropriate bicycle and changing rooms. Whatever the precise range of services, the cost will fall on the tenants through service charge except to the extent that any tenant excludes identified items of service expenditure.

6.41 In Chapter 9 (para 9.53) the CRC Energy Efficiency Scheme is discussed. In multi-occupancy developments, the most obvious method of dealing with the CRC is through service charge but many current leases would not have the inherent flexibility to enable landlords to recover the CRC costs. The cost of purchasing allowances may have to be borne by landlords and few tenants would agree to a lease variation. Nor are new leases free from problems such as:

- Tenants cannot ensure the compliance of landlords and penalties imposed on landlords should not be paid by tenants;

- The cost of purchasing allowances fluctuates with time and poor decisions by landlords could inflate the costs funded through service charge;

- With the CRC applying to group properties tenants of an energy efficient development could be subsidising less efficient properties in the portfolio; tenants will argue for site-specific participation;

- Timing issues may arise due to a mismatch among the dates for purchasing allowances, receiving RRP and the service charge year;

- How is the RRP to be reimbursed to tenants.

6.42 That said, solutions to these problems are likely to emerge with time and there seems to be evidence that, in the office market, some enthusiasm for green leases is developing. Tenants may be alive to the possibility that, although CRC costs may increase service charge, they may open doors to negotiating opportunities elsewhere, including on rent review (para 8.79) and, of course, there is pressure on all parties to reduce energy costs.

Chapter 7

Insurance and Related Matters

TYPES OF INSURANCE

7.1 Clauses covering various types of insurance (and the cost) and closely related matters like *rei interitus*, rent abatement and early termination, although often distributed throughout the lease, require unified consideration. Landlords may require insurance against:

(i)   property owner's liability, third party liability and employer's liability;

(ii)   plate glass damage;

(iii)   mechanical and electrical breakdown etc affecting plant and machinery in so far as not covered by (v);

(iv)   miscellaneous matters such as staff vehicle insurance or sprinkler leakage;

(v)   damage or destruction of the subjects of lease or any larger development of which they form a part;

(vi)   loss of rent and possibly service charge.

7.2 The landlord's solicitor must ensure that the lease contains, whether grouped together or singly, provisions requiring payment by the tenant of the costs of these insurances, apportioned when necessary among various tenants (see para 4.18). Items (i)–(iv) are self-explanatory although the obligation upon the tenant (the others are insured by the landlord) to insure against plate glass damage is often waived by a back letter personal to the tenant (paras 2.32–2.36). Items (v) and (vi), by contrast, raise important considerations. However, in looking at the following relevant issues, parties should bear in mind that in the institutional form of lease the property insurance is an extension of the underlying obligation upon the tenant of total responsibility for the physical condition of the subjects of lease and of joint financial responsibility with the other tenants for the common parts. To the extent that insurance money is not available (unless consequent on a contractual breach by the landlord) the tenant has to repair or rebuild (or pay proportionately in respect of common parts) from its own resources.

7.3 The lease must cover these components of property insurance:
- (i)   who insures and in what name;
- (ii)   the status of potential insurers;
- (iii)   the basis for the sum insured;
- (iv)   identification of risks and other contract terms;

leading then to detailed matters linked to rebuilding.

WHO INSURES

7.4 Rarely is the tenant allowed to insure although sometimes a private landlord of a single property will allow a powerful tenant to do so, usually by back letter. The impracticality of insuring the subjects of lease separately from other parts of a building in the ownership of the landlord and, more generally, concerns about protection of the landlord's investment (to avoid non-insurance, to exercise control over insurance proceeds and possibly to extract some financial benefits (para 4.18)), will dictate that the landlord insures as would obligations to that effect either contained in a development lease in which the landlord is the tenant or imposed in loan documentation where the landlord has used the subjects of lease as security. This should be expressed as an obligation to insure and keep insured, not that of paying premiums or similar. Given that the landlord is insuring, these issues of control arise:

7.5 Insurance in the joint names of the landlord and the tenant results in joint control of the proceeds and of the reinstatement, avoids difficulties with subrogation rights (para 7.6) and offers protection to the tenant from potential liquidation of the landlord. However, as with the tenant's insurance, it is impractical where the subjects of lease are part of a larger development, there may be controls already imposed in a superior lease or loan documentation and in consequence, whatever the apparent benefits to the tenant, few landlords will accept reductions in control. Rarely, therefore, does the landlord insure in joint names.

7.6 However, landlords do often accept that the interest of the tenant should be endorsed on the policy (whether or not it relates to more than the subjects of lease) either specifically or generically. This puts the insurance company on notice that there is an interest in the policy separate from the landlord's and when the noting is specific it is likely that the insurance company would notify the tenant were the policy to lapse. This procedure can also reduce the opportunity for the insurer, having settled a claim, to stand in the shoes of the landlord and pursue the tenant, alleging that the damage was caused by an act or omission of the tenant in breach of the lease, although it is in any event doubtful if the pursuit of these so-called subrogation rights would be successful where the tenant had been paying the premium[1]. Because some doubt remains it has become common for tenants to ask landlords to produce from the insurers a specific waiver of subrogation rights. Landlords (who have no particular axe to grind) regularly do so but should avoid an unqualified obligation as insurers and market conditions change over time.

1   *Mark Rowlands Ltd v Berni Inns Ltd and Ors* [1986] 1 QB 211; *Barras v Hamilton* 1994 SLT 949, 1994 SCLR 700.

STATUS OF INSURERS

7.7 The status of the insurers is relevant in relation to the ready availability of funds in the event of a claim and possibly also on premium levels discussed in paragraph 4.18. Although commercial landlords are sometimes themselves part of an insurance group, generally they accept that the insurers be stated to be of good repute and with a substantial presence in the United Kingdom, this being designed to reduce practical difficulties in the event of a claim.

SUMS INSURED

7.8 The principle underlying insurance is that of indemnification for loss[1], usually based on market value. However, that principle can be varied by the insurance contract to provide insurance funds, in the event of total destruction, to rebuild the property and although the landlord may in some circumstances prefer to redevelop the property rather than rebuild (para

7.14), it is usual for the lease to provide for insurance for reinstatement value or preferably for the full cost of reinstatement (including professional fees, demolition, debris removal etc plus VAT on the foregoing) which might properly be expected to be incurred where reinstatement takes place. That may be years later where there are difficulties over permissions or if a complex building is involved. The ascertainment of that cost (including the inflationary element) will not be a simple matter, particularly as changing building techniques and regulations allied to planning requirements (including those for listed buildings) may combine to require the reinstated building to differ markedly from its predecessor (para 7.14). Upon this subject, therefore, the landlord needs assistance from insurance advisers. For their part (and with an eye for the discussion on shortfall (para 7.14)) tenants are usually content for the landlord to control the sum insured, possibly constrained by 'fair and reasonable'.

---

1   *Carrick Furniture House Ltd v General Accident, Fire and Life Assurance Corpn Ltd* 1977 SC 308, 1978 SLT 65 (OH).

RISKS

7.9 Because of its underlying obligation to fund rebuilding costs, the tenant needs certainty on the risks covered. Definitions structured to allow the landlord total discretion create obvious dangers for the tenant. It is preferable to include a list of identified risks against which both parties would want cover and provide for additional cover against which the landlord, acting reasonably, thinks it advisable to insure and having regard to any reasonable representations made by the tenant. However, in agreeing to this, the landlord should ensure that:

- the lease provides that the tenant bears all normal commercial excesses;

- all cover is subject to such limitations and exclusions as may be imposed from time to time by the insurers, for example, in relation to vacant property.

7.10 The parties also need to contemplate circumstances in which cover at reasonable rates and conditions may not always be available for all of the identified risks, the most obvious being an act of terrorism. Many landlords now accept liability for these risks and will also abate rent as for other risks that are covered, provided that there is a right for the landlord to terminate the lease where damage to the subjects of lease (or common parts) makes them unfit for full beneficial use. In coming to this position the tenant requires to ensure that damage by such risks is excluded from the direct and indirect repair clauses (paras 5.16 and 6.15); the precise wording of such exclusions is dependant on the lease definitions, but 'Uninsured Risks' is frequently used. For its part, the landlord needs to ensure that the loss of rent insurance applies to these circumstances.

7.11 The foregoing demonstrates the need for co-operation between parties with similar concerns and prompts a further requirement. The landlord will require a clause (usually within the tenant's general obligations and thereby remote from the insurance clause) obliging the tenant to comply with the terms of the insurance policy and specifically to avoid partial or total vitiation or increased premiums (although, on this latter point, tenants may argue that they should not be in breach if they pay the additional premiums). That, combined with a need to be satisfied that the landlord is in full compliance with its obligations, demands a clause whereby the landlord provides evidence of the existing terms of the policy coupled with an obligation of timeous disclosure of material changes and premium receipts. Tenants prefer that, in questions of liability with their landlord, any changes to the policy are deemed effective only from intimation. In order generally to satisfy their obligation under a clause of the kind described, major landlords with portfolio insurance would wish, instead of providing a copy of the policy, to provide evidence of its terms and of its being in force. Knowledge of the terms of the insurance policy current from time to time, including the spread of risk, also enables a tenant in the absence of any prohibition in the lease to that effect to insure risks for which the landlord has been unable to provide cover.

7.12 Paragraphs 7.4 to 7.11 are concerned with the terms of the property insurance necessary to protect the respective interests and obligations of the parties under the lease. The occurrence of damage to the subjects of lease or the common parts raises in turn a number of very important considerations, not all of which appear superficially to be linked in the lease.

7.13 As we saw in paragraph 5.10 the doctrine of *rei interitus* provides for the automatic termination of a lease where the subjects of lease are totally destroyed or so damaged as to prevent the intended use[1]. The contract can also be frustrated by such events as compulsory acquisition or requisition[2]. However, service by a planning authority of an enforcement notice preventing the intended use of the subjects of lease is not a supervening event and the contract continues[3] thereby emphasising the need for the tenant to check the authorised planning use before commitment (para 9.33). Our common law also provides for rent abatement, whole or partial, dependent on circumstances. Such principles, which many would argue are sensible and fair, are unacceptable to commercial landlords (many of whom are familiar with the English system) intent on preserving an income stream and modern leases overcome them by express provisions that:

- the lease continues notwithstanding damage or destruction. From the landlord's perspective, it is preferable to site that clause outwith the insurance provisions to avoid any implication (or, worse, specific drafting) which restricts the relevant circumstances to insured risk damage alone;

- rent is paid for the entire duration without deduction except (possibly) any required by law;

- there is abatement of rent only in limited defined circumstances (para 7.15).

---

1   *Cantors Properties (Scotland) Ltd v Swears and Wells Ltd* 1978 SC 310, 1980 SLT 165.
2   *Mackeson v Boyd* 1942 SC 56, 1942 SLT 106; *Fehilly v General Accident Fire and Life Assurance Corporation Ltd* 1983 SLT 141.
3   *Robert Purvis Plant Hire Ltd v Brewster* [2009] CSOH 28.

Restoration and Shortfall

7.14 It may be thought that the inclusion of the detailed insurance provisions of the type discussed in this chapter, combined with those in paragraph 7.13 intended to allow the survival of the lease on major damage, and the exclusion from both the direct repairing clause (para 5.16) or any service charge provision (para 6.15) of any obligations on the tenant to repair insured risk damage would be followed inexorably by requirements upon the landlord (save in respect of vitiation and relative to the operation of excesses) to restore expeditiously all insured risk damage. This is not so for a variety of reasons:

- a few leases omit completely any obligation by the landlord to reinstate. This is wholly unsatisfactory to the tenant who is deprived of the benefit of *rei interitus* and common-law rent abatement, is given in substitution a limited period of abatement and has no easy method of forcing either reinstatement or termination of the lease;

- a landlord, possibly where the property is old, may anticipate redevelopment (towards the cost of which it would have insurance proceeds) by including an option to terminate on the occurrence of insured risk damage. If disposed to consider this, a tenant should limit the clause to material damage, require early exercise of the option (failing which total reinstatement by the landlord takes place), limit the exercise of the option to the later years of the lease and try to share in the insurance proceeds (para 7.17);

- many leases limit the landlord's obligation of reinstatement to the spending of the insurance proceeds. But what if there is a shortfall? Few would deny that a landlord, in total control of the insurance of the subjects of let including the sum insured, should be responsible for any shortfall (save in respect of vitiation and excluding excesses) and thereby accept responsibility for the consequences of its own actions. It should be remembered that the tenant has limited input to the insurance beyond paying the premiums and perhaps a fee to the landlord for insurance valuations designed to assist the landlord in avoiding underinsurance. On an associated matter, the tenant should resist an obligation to value its fitting-out works for the landlord's insurance purposes but should provide details of the cost (para 2.29);

- controls such as planning permission, conservation area consent, listed building consent and building regulations may conspire to prevent a like-for-like replacement and indeed neither landlord nor tenant may want that. Landlords should ensure that the drafting does not require an identical restoration provided that the tenant is given back property which is substantially equivalent to the original. Of course, it may be that in this whole area of major damage and reinstatement, a measure of sensible commercial compromise among parties is necessary.

Abatement

7.15 The contractual abatement clause to replace our common law has been referred to on a number of occasions. The following features require consideration.

- Will the abatement cover only rent (as properly defined) or also service charge? In a multi-occupancy development where only some properties are so damaged as to prevent occupation, substantial service charge liabilities will continue. The abatement is sometimes extended to service charge, provided that it falls within the insurance provision. Very rarely would a landlord abate the liability of a tenant if not reimbursed from proceeds of an insurance policy (the premiums on which are paid by the tenant).

- Usually rent/service charge abatement will apply only where occupancy is deprived due to an insured risk but needs to be extended to cover identified risks for which cover may not be available (para 7.10). The tenant may have to accept that the emergence of, say, latent defects or planning restrictions, either of which could prevent occupation and trading, does not trigger abatement.

- The tenant should ensure that abatement operates when deprivation of proper occupancy rights is triggered by damage to common parts, not just the subjects of lease.

- It is usual for disputes about the period or proportion of abatement to be determined by an expert.

- Landlords often 'cap' the abatement to the period for which loss of rent insurance is available or, worse still from the tenant's angle, to the sums actually received. In the first case, delays in reinstatement can leave the tenant paying rent while deprived of occupation. In the second case, additionally the tenant would be liable for a shortfall in insurance proceeds if the landlord had itself vitiated the policy or, more likely, underestimated the rent where the period straddled a review date. The tenant's position is that the landlord is in control of reinstatement due to insured risk damage and no rent should be paid during a period in which the tenant is deprived of occupation. In practice, however, few tenants wish to remain contractually bound for years, awaiting reinstatement. Most would prefer our common law to apply rather than take up short-term lets, possibly of less suitable property, for uncertain periods until able to return. Particular difficulties exist for retailers in this scenario. It is therefore common for tenants to insist that, in respect of reinstatement, landlords use all reasonable endeavours to obtain the necessary permissions and with all expedition thereafter complete the reinstatement but that failure by the landlord to do so within an agreed period (no longer than the period covered by loss of rent insurance) allows either party (but not the landlord if in breach) to terminate the lease on one month's notice.

7.16 The last element of insurance is item (vi), namely that for loss of rent and possibly service charge. As already mentioned, this insurance is intended by the landlord to replace the income excluded by the abatement clause. Provided that the landlord ensures that such insurance covers all situations in which abatement could be triggered and that it avoids underestimating the insured sums, the clause should fulfil its stated objective.

OWNERSHIP OF FUNDS

7.17 Finally, on insurance, the lease should settle the ownership of the insurance funds if reinstatement is not effected, because the landlord either has no obligation to reinstate or is prevented from doing so. There is some English case law suggesting that the proceeds should be divided between the parties according to their respective interests. It should also be recognised that the tenant does have a property interest, having (possibly) spent large sums of money fitting out a developer's shell, which expenditure may not have been amortised. That said, very few leases are settled on the basis of a sharing of proceeds and where the issue is narrated (as is recommended), usually the landlord is stated to be entitled to retain the full proceeds from the insurance policies.

Chapter 8

Rent Review

OBJECTIVE

8.1 The common theme of numerous judicial descriptions of the purpose of rent review clauses is that of reflecting changes in the value of money and property likely to occur during a lease. Despite various market trends over time which have seen the emergence of alternative ways of realising that purpose and which are discussed in paragraphs 8.68–8.78, by far the most common method remains that which allows the rent to be reviewed at certain dates by reference to the open market rent of the subjects of lease. Almost universally, this is on an 'upward only' basis, by which strictly is meant that at review the rent will not go down as the rent at each review is stated to be the higher of the current rent and the open market rent as determined. A few leases substitute the starting rent for the current rent in that comparison, so that the rent on review can never fall below the original rent. That simply stated objective has, over time, produced increasingly sophisticated clauses spawning many court cases and a degree of angst among property lawyers at the potential of such clauses to produce unexpected and unwelcome results. Although well advised parties, having learned the lessons from many past disputes, now tend to adopt a more conciliatory approach to the adjustment of rent review clauses, and there are now few court challenges in comparison to past years, both new and existing clauses still demand care.

8.2 Rent review clauses have four principal elements, namely:
- (i)   the mechanics for implementing the review,
- (ii)   the criteria for determining the rent after review,
- (iii) third party determination provisions and,
- (iv)   procedural matters.

THE MECHANICS OF IMPLEMENTATION

The Review Date(s)

8.3 The traditional duration of 25 years has now been replaced with 10 or 15 years and break options are common (para 8.42). One review date only is no longer rare in leases currently being granted. Those responsible for drafting should opt for clarity and certainty. Precise dates should be preferred to formulae such as '28 May in every fifth year'. Where the property is not completed at the time of adjustment of the lease, the agreement for lease needs to provide a clear formula, eg 'on the 5th, 10th, 15th and 20th anniversaries of the date of entry', with blanks in the draft lease for insertion of precise dates in the engrossment. Formulae designed to ensure that, for management reasons, the review date(s) fall(s) on quarter days mean either an acceleration of the date(s) (unfavourable generally to the tenant) or deferment (less favourable to the landlord).

8.4 The originally planned review date(s) should usually be those relevant both to the level of rent and to the uplift[1] but certain circumstances could dictate otherwise. Either way, the drafting should be clear. Different dates for level and uplift are sometimes provided as a fallback position for the landlord who is late in reviewing (para 8.12).

---

1   See eg *Accuba Ltd v Allied Shoe Repairs Ltd* [1975], 1 WLR 1559, 3 All ER 782.

8.5 The current rent review pattern for most leases remains at five years. This is significant in valuation terms (para 8.43) and, although other periods such as 3 years are not uncommon (and some extant leases have a less frequent pattern), unusual patterns create difficulty with comparables. In leases exceeding 25 years, the landlord may be concerned that the review clause which is central to its investment value may, over time, fail to protect it because either the conventional pattern alters or such clauses change materially. This is an understandable concern, but clauses which anticipate this fear by providing for a review of the pattern or even of the whole clause could work to the landlord's disadvantage and options to change exercisable by the landlord alone are so patently disadvantageous to the tenant as to provoke resistance.

8.6 Most modern commercial leases provide that, after each of the planned review dates, the rent shall be the open market rent (or, if higher, the existing rent), that rent (if not agreed by the parties) to be determined on the application of landlord or tenant by an independent third party. This is a contract between landlord and tenant to the effect that rent reviews will take place at agreed dates and that, failing agreement, either may refer the matter to third party determination. The procedure avoids the need for 'trigger notices' and, as will be discussed in the next paragraph, the uncertainties and unfairness inherent therein.

The 'trigger' for review

8.7 Despite the present unpopularity of such clauses, many older leases still in operation (and a few still being granted) do not include the contractual style of review described in paragraph 8.6. They contain clauses where, to initiate the review, the landlord has to serve a notice in a particular timescale and the tenant, to avoid implied acceptance of the proposed rent contained in the notice, is obliged to serve a counter-notice timeously. This procedure raises difficult problems, many of which feature the issue of whether time is of the essence.

Time of the Essence

8.8 In England the general rule was laid down by the House of Lords in *United Scientific Holdings v Burnley Borough Council*[1] to the effect that, unless the lease expressly says otherwise or it can be inferred from the whole circumstances that the parties intended otherwise, strict time compliance is not presumed. In Scotland the position was clarified by *Visionhire Ltd v Britel Fund Trustees Ltd*[2] in which Lord President Hope reviewed the authorities in both jurisdictions. He concluded that there is no significant difference between the two countries.

However, his Lordship gave two specific examples where time would be of the essence, namely (a) where a party who had been subject to unreasonable delay gives notice to the other party and stipulates that time is of the essence and (b) where the review clause itself provides for certain consequences in the absence of steps being taken within a certain time. Thus, although the presumption is against time being of the essence, the drafting of the lease and the actings of the parties are capable of overturning it. One presumes that the general principle of *Visionhire Ltd v Britel Fund Trustees Ltd* would enable a landlord, caught by a mandatory period as in *Yates Petitioner*[3] which would render a notice invalid if not served on a precise date, to serve another trigger notice.

1   *United Scientific Holdings v Burnley Borough Council* [1978] AC 904.
2   *Visionhire Ltd v Britel Fund Trustees Ltd* 1991 SLT 883.
3   *Yates Petitioner* 1987 SLT 86.

8.9 A landlord who, because of an administrative error, loses for a period of years its 'right' to obtain the open market rent for its property is heavily penalised and that prospect alone will impact adversely on the value of its investment. Such is the penalty that the landlord's solicitor must resist any drafting which would have the effect, expressly or impliedly, of making time of the essence in any part of the procedure, except on the clearest instruction from a well-advised and knowledgeable client.

8.10 Even although inaccurate or inconsistent drafting can still produce areas of doubt[1], the effect of express drafting should be clear. In contrast, drafting from which it can be inferred that the parties intended that time be of the essence is more uncertain. Such drafting may result from a disguised effort by the tenant's solicitor to protect his/her client and an incomplete understanding by his/her counterpart of the potential effect of wording which was assumed to have a more limited (or different) purpose.

1   *Wrenbridge Ltd v Harries (Southern Properties) Ltd* (1981) 260 EG 1195; *Wilderbrook v Oluwu* [2005] EWCA Cir 1361.

8.11 The importance to the landlord (and to the tenant in the counter-notice procedure discussed at paragraph 8.16) demands clarity. In the unusual circumstances in which the parties agree that time is of the essence, it must be preferable to state this clearly and expressly[1] (and by reference to the appropriate step or steps concerned) rather than rely upon contra-indications.

---

1   *C Richards & Sons Ltd v Karenita Ltd* (1972) 221 EG 25.

8.12 One such contra-indication is where the review clause provides specifically for certain consequences in the absence of action within the timetable. Commonly this allows the landlord, failing its timeous service of the rent review notice, to review late on a further period of notice. Usually the level of rent will be that appropriate to the originally planned review date, with the uplift applied from the later date. By this contractual solution, the parties agree to limit the damage to the landlord caused by its administrative failure.

8.13 Many forms of contra-indication turn on the precise words and circumstances of the case at issue and it is doubtful if much is to be gained from an attempt to reach any clear conclusion from the plethora of cases, sometimes appearing to produce conflicting results, that have come before the (English) courts. By way of example, the words 'if the Landlord shall so require by notice in writing given to the Tenant within three months thereafter but not otherwise'[1] have been held to make time of the essence whereas 'shall as soon as practicable and in any event not later than three months after service of the said notice ...'[2] have produced the opposite result. Later cases provide limited assistance save to emphasise the point (admittedly of little help when dealing with existing leases so framed) that it is preferable to draw rent review clauses in the contractual style or, if there are to be periods, to state clearly and expressly where time is to be of the essence.

---

1   *Drebbond Ltd v Horsham District Council* (1978) 246 EG 1013; (1979) 37 P&CR 237.
2   *Touche Ross & Co v Secretary of State for the Environment* (1982) 265 EG 982.

8.14 The same conclusion can be reached when considering another potential contra-indication, namely the existence of a break clause. In

United Scientific Holdings v Burnley Borough Council[1] the House of Lords had expressly approved the terms of the rent review clause in the lease examined in *C Richards & Sons Ltd v Karenita Ltd*[2] as an example of where time should be of the essence. There the review, triggered by a landlord's notice only, was upward only and was followed by a period for the tenant to decide whether to serve a notice of termination. The law in England on this issue was reviewed in *Central Estates Ltd v Secretary of State for the Environment*[3] where the Court of Appeal held that there was in that case a sufficiently clear correlation between the provisions of the break clause and the rent review clause to make time of the essence. However, close correlation of timetabling is not always sufficient to rebut the presumption where, for example, the event (as to which time was argued to be of the essence) was outwith the landlord's control or the tenant could have taken the initiative on rent review[4].

1   *United Scientific Holdings v Burnley Borough Council* [1978] AC 904
2   *C Richards & Sons Ltd v Karenita Ltd* (1972) 221 EG 25.
3   *Central Estates Ltd v Secretary of State for the Environment* [1995] EGCS 110.
4   *Metrolands Investment Ltd v J H Dewhurst Ltd* (1985) 1 EGLR 105.

8.15 Until now we have been considering the dangers of notice procedures from the perspective of the landlord. Consideration has also to be given to the form of clause which invites a tenant's counter-notice within a stated period (often 21 days), failing which the rent proposed in the landlord's notice is deemed to be agreed. Such clauses are common in the type of rent review clause which contains notice procedures and are still being introduced into contractual rent review clauses by some landlords anxious to punish tenants for any delay.

8.16 The dangers for the tenant are clear. An administrative failure could result in payment by the tenant for the whole of the subsequent review period (and beyond that in a depressed market, given an upward-only review clause) of a rent which, advanced by the landlord as a negotiating rent, may greatly exceed the true open market rent. Reasonable landlords accept that an administrative oversight should deprive neither the landlord of the right to review nor the tenant of its right to be heard in the review process. For these reasons, if faced with such a clause, the tenant's solicitor should, failing complete excision, sanitise it by requiring that failure to respond equals a deemed rejection of the landlord's proposal, thus triggering third party determination.

8.17 However, while these clauses remain in some leases, the courts will continue to be exercised by their terms. The normal rules on time of the essence apply but there are difficulties in the application of the general principle. In a comparatively recent case of this kind to come before the English courts, time was held not to be of the essence, although the decision was reached with some reluctance and invited an appeal. The Court of Appeal reversed the decision.[1] This has a measure of consistency with two earlier Scottish cases where the unwary tenant suffered[2]. The difficulty for the practitioner is that the distinctions drawn are so fine as to defy rational analysis, lending support to the proposition that such counter-notice procedures should be resisted or that proper drafting should remove any doubt.

1   *Starmark Enterprises Ltd v CPL Distribution Ltd* [2001] EWCA Cir 1252
2   *Charterhouse Square Finance Co Ltd v A & J Menswear Ltd* 1998 SLT 720; *Scottish Life Assurance Co Ltd v Agfa–Gevaert Ltd* 1998 SC 171, 1998 SLT 481, 1998 SCLR 238.

8.18 Consideration has to be given to the impact on the rent review mechanism, as a whole, of failure by the landlord timeously to implement an element in the clause where time is of the essence. If time is not of the essence generally, can the landlord simply start the whole process again? In *Norwich Union Life Insurance Society v Sketchley plc*[1] the court held that, on the precise words before it, the chance for review came once only. With the same style of lease, the court in another case reached the very opposite conclusion[2].

1   *Norwich Union Life Insurance Society v Sketchley plc* [1986] 2 EGLR 130; 280 EG 773.
2   *Norwich Union Life Insurance Society v Tony Waller Ltd* (1984) 270 EG 42.

8.19 That these provisions often appear to give to the landlord the exclusive right to serve the notice triggering review have led, usually where the review is open (ie not upward only), to attempts by the tenant to persuade the courts to force the landlord to progress the review. The courts have held that there is no presumption that machinery of this nature must be activated at each review, or that it ought to be capable of exercise by both parties; rather it is a matter of construction of the terms of the lease as a whole[1] In *Royal Bank of Scotland plc v Jennings and Others*[2], the court held that the notice provisions were machinery to allow the implementation of reviews which, from its terms, the lease intended to happen and that the court was entitled to supply machinery to avoid frustration of that outcome. In *Hemingway Realty Ltd v Clothworkers Company*[3] the court concluded that the lease clearly provided an exclusive right to review to the landlord and this had to be given effect. It may be observed that, presuming a review clause with trigger notice provisions, the easier course certainly where the review is open is to allow both parties to pull that trigger.

---

1   See remarks of Lord Fraser in United Scientific Holdings (supra) at 961C.
2   *Royal Bank of Scotland plc v Jennings and Others* (1998) 75 P&CR 458.
3   *Hemingway Realty Ltd v Clothworkers Co* [2006] EWHC 299.

8.20 As mentioned earlier (para 8.12), rent review clauses of the notice variety sometimes provide a specific remedy for late review, namely that the landlord can review to the level appropriate at the original review date and uplift from the date of expiry of the late review notice period. Where no such provision appears and time is not of the essence, the uplift would operate from the original rent review date[1]. Arguably, this is unfair to the tenant, particularly if combined with a penalty rate of interest (para 8.65) and it is a subject to which the courts have directed attention.

---

1   *C H Bailey Ltd v Memorial Enterprises Ltd* [1974] 1 All ER 1003.

8.21 The early cases[1] favoured tenants in denying landlords the right to review some years later than the contractual date but later (English) cases have come gradually to the position where delay, however lengthy, does not destroy the contractual right[2]. Personal bar may offer some comfort to the tenant, although the English courts would seem to be more reluctant than those in Scotland to provide this remedy. In *Banks v Mecca Bookmakers*

(Scotland) Ltd[3], followed in *Waydale Ltd v MRM Engineering*[4], the landlord failed in a retrospective rent review following on collection of rents at the old rate well after the date of review, a case which has led to the universal inclusion in leases by well-advised landlords of a provision that demand for and/or acceptance of rent at the old rate after review will not constitute a waiver of the right to review.

---

1   See eg *Telegraph Properties (Securities) Ltd v Courtaulds* (1981) 257 EG 1153.
2   *Amherst v James Walker Goldsmith & Silversmith Ltd* (No 2) [1983] Ch 305.
3   *Banks v Mecca Bookmakers (Scotland) Ltd* 1982 SC7, SLT 150.
4   *Waydale Ltd v M R M Engineering* 1995 GWD 23–1263.

Administrative Problems

8.22 Aside from the central question of whether time is of the essence in trigger notices and counter-notices, there are a number of related traps for the unwary and it follows that care should be taken by the parties to ensure that notices are served within the contractual timescale, upon the appropriate party at the correct address and in accordance with all other relevant provisions of the lease. Among the administrative issues debated in court are the following:

8.23 In general the courts in recent times have taken account of commercial reality and, whether in respect of trigger notices or counter-notices, have avoided an overly pedantic approach[1].

---

1   See eg *Nunes and anor v Davies Laing & Dick* (1985) 51 P&CR 310; *Prudential Property Services Ltd v Capital Land Holdings Ltd* [1993] 1 EGLR 128.

8.24 Some leases require the tenant to elect for third party determination if it disagrees with the rent proposed in the trigger notice; in these circumstances the tenant should ensure that not only is the proposed rent rejected but the reference to the third party is clear[1].

---

1   See eg *Edlingham Ltd v MFI Furniture Centres Ltd* (1981) 259 EG 421.

8.25 Many leases provide that the landlord's trigger notice should specify the proposed rent. There are two English cases which provide differing results in the absence of such a proposal[1,] although it is thought that only rarely would the requirement be held to be mandatory[2]. It is not entirely clear whether the level of rent proposed must be reasonable[3] but it seems unlikely that a Scottish court would wish to intervene in that judgment, given that the tenant has the option of serving a counter-notice.

1   *Dean and Chapter of Chichester Cathedral v Lennards Ltd* (1977) 244 EG 807; *Commission for the New Towns v R Levy & Co Ltd* (1990) 28 EG 119.
2   *Patel v Earlspring Properties Ltd* [1991] 2 EGLR 131.
3   See *Davstone (Holdings) Ltd v Al-Rifai* (1976) 32 P&CR 18; *Amalgamated Estates Ltd v Joystretch Manufacturing Ltd* (1980) 257 EG 489, [1981] 1 EGLR 96; *Earl of Stradbrook v Mitchell* (1991) 03 EG 128, [1991] 1 EGLR 1.

8.26 The introduction into notices and counter-notices of 'without prejudice' or the English phrase 'subject to contract' serves only to muddy the waters of what may sometimes be a very murky pool but where, as mentioned in paragraph 8.23, the general trend is to save the notice (or counter-notice) if the ordinary recipient could understand its purpose. Contrasting results are found in many cases on this matter[1].

1   *Shirlcar Properties Ltd v Heinitz* (1983) 268 EG 362; *Norwich Union Life Assurance Society v Tony Waller Ltd* (1984) 270 EG 42; *Sheridan v Blaircourt Investments* (1984) 270 EG 1290; but see also *British Rail Pensions Trustees Co Ltd v Cardshops* [1987] 1 EGLR 127 and *Royal Life Insurance v Phillips* [1990] 43 EG 70.

REVIEW CRITERIA

General

8.27 Although other methods of reviewing rent may be increasing in popularity and in sub-leases rents at review may be directly related to those in their head leases, most leases use an open market rent approach. In essence, this requires a consideration of rents paid for comparable properties adjusted to circumstances including the terms of the relevant leases (but see para 8.78).

8.28 Accordingly, the definition of 'open market rent' (or similar phrase) inserted in leases proceeds on a hypothesis, namely that the subjects of lease are let on the open market at the review date. This requires an assumption that the subjects are vacant (para 8.34) and that a willing landlord and (possibly) willing tenant exist (para 8.38) but most leases then tilt the balance between actual and hypothetical firmly towards the latter by incorporating assumptions and disregards which, over time, have become increasingly detailed.

8.29 Examples of the hypothetical components of rent review clauses contained in modern leases are considered later but, in general, any movement from actual to hypothetical should be considered with caution. Experience suggests that even skilled draftsmen, armed with proper instructions from their clients and their surveyors (and modern commercial pressures often militate against that counsel of perfection), may fail to anticipate all the consequences of the envisaged departure from reality. Courts, facing increasingly bizarre results, have tended to seek refuge in identifying the underlying commercial purpose which, in itself, may be taken as presuming actual, not hypothetical, terms, assuming the absence of clear contra-indications[1]. Nevertheless in any particular case the decision may be very different from that expected by either or both of the parties. Such an unwelcome result may also face the tenant who has allowed the landlord, by the copious use of assumptions and disregards, to invent a hypothetical lease much less onerous than the actual lease and thereby capable of commanding a materially enhanced rent.

---

1   *Basingstoke and Deane Borough Council v Host Group Ltd* [1988] 1 All ER 824.

Definition of Open Market Rent

8.30 Although there are many styles, the definition proposed by the landlord is likely to be along these lines:

(a)   'the best [or 'rack' or 'open market' or similar] yearly rent for which the Subjects of Lease with the benefit of the Common Rights [or similar] could reasonably be expected to be let as a whole (or, if greater, in parts notwithstanding the provision for sub-letting herein contained) with vacant possession on the

Relevant Review Date in the open market by a willing landlord to a willing tenant without premium for a duration equal to the original duration of this lease upon the terms and conditions (excluding rent) as are herein contained ...'

This section of the definition comprises elements which, it may be argued, are reasonably required to put into operation the hypothesis of a lease of the property on the open market at the review date. These are considered in paragraphs 8.31–8.43.

    (b)   'and on the assumption that, if not a fact, ...'

There then follows a list of specific assumptions intended to prevent any acts or omissions of the tenant or authorised occupier from lowering the rent. These are considered in paragraphs 8.44–8.50.

    (c)   'but there being disregarded ...'

These specific disregards are intended to prevent the rent from being increased due to the efforts (or indeed presence) in the property of the tenant and its predecessors in title. These are considered in paragraphs 8.51–8.55.

In practice, the distinction in objective between assumptions and disregards is ignored by many draftsmen, particularly by those who reverse some of the assumptions and re-express them also as disregards.

The Basic Elements in paragraph (a)

8.31 Definitions of the term Open Market Rent or Market Rent, (the latter being the term used in the Appraisal and Valuation Manual of the Royal Institution of Chartered Surveyors commonly called the 'Red Book'), often start with words like 'best', 'fair' or 'rack' which provoke concern. Some worry that 'best' may admit the extreme valuation of a special bidder, 'fair' may imply an element of subjectivity and 'rack' may connote the maximum rent permitted by law[1]. It is questionable if these fears are justified but the safest course may be to resist the inclusion of all such words and rely on the defined term itself.

---

1   *Compton Group Ltd v Estates Gazette Ltd* (1977) 244 EG 799.

8.32 The Subjects of Lease. Usually, the subjects of the hypothetical lease are the actual subjects and no special difficulties arise if these have been precisely defined along with rights and reservations and clarity, so far as rent review is concerned, on tenant's improvements and fixtures and fittings (para 8.54). But if the tenant enjoys the property in association with other property held under a different lease or licence or agreement which provides significant facilities (eg access, fire escape, car parking), the landlord must, in the rent review clause, assume the existence of these or alternative rights, otherwise the hypothetical tenant would be stripped of these facilities. And if the ancillary document is granted by the landlord, it should incorporate these rights for the purposes of the rent review. However, even then the subjects of lease can move from the actual to the hypothetical in two ways:

(i)   It is sometimes argued, particularly where the subjects are unusual and give rise to measurement disputes, that an assumed floor area stated in the lease would avoid subsequent and regular arguments at each review. In pre-lets, this dictates that the agreement provides a formula for insertion of this agreed assumed area in the lease. But difficulties exist. An arbiter may have to fix a rent for a property with a stated assumed floor area which he cannot understand or justify or whose original method of calculation is unavailable or where the Code of Measuring Practice (upon which comparables are based) has changed or where the subjects have been physically altered with any licence being silent on rent review. In any of these circumstances, apparent certainty may have been gained at the price of fairness to one of the parties.

(ii)   If the subjects of lease are an unusual building and/or in an unusual location, an absence of proper comparables should be anticipated in the drafting. If, despite such difficulties, parties opt for an open market review based on comparables, very careful drafting is required. Such was the problem in *Dukeminster (Ebbgate House One) Ltd v Somerfield Properties Co Ltd*[1] where an unusual building (a warehouse of 250,000 square feet) was built in an odd location (Ross-on-Wye). The lease provided that the rent be geared to notional warehouse premises of 50,000 square feet within a 35-mile radius of Ross-on-Wye but neglected to be more precise on location despite wide rental variations within the selected geographical circle. The spectrum of possibilities argued ranged from the clause being void from uncertainty to the landlord being able to select the area producing the highest rent. On appeal, all previous efforts at interpretation were discarded in favour of what the court considered the parties must have intended. This was that, in the absence of any 250,000 square feet warehouses anywhere or of 50,000 square feet units in Ross-on-Wye, the valuer could consider the whole of the designated area but only if the locations were comparable to Ross-on-Wye. This is not a forensic triumph and reinforces the point that movement from actual to hypothetical must be accompanied by prescient drafting, a hard lesson learned by the landlord in *Scottish Mutual Association Society v Secretary of State for the Environment*[2]. The drafting should be very specific on location and building specification and assumptions about ancillary rights such as car parking may be necessary. If the hypothetical building is described as 'modern' it would be best from the perspective of the landlord where the lease is to endure for many years to put beyond doubt that this assumed description would apply at each review, thereby providing a form of automatic updating. Nevertheless, despite such efforts, there remains a risk of a distortion of valuation caused by importing such an abnormal clause into the valuation hypothesis. This type of difficulty, associated also with a question of user, was considered in *McDonalds Real Estate LLP v Arundel Corp*[3] where the lease provided for an alternative for review of a 'modern single storey warehouse', the actual building being a drive-through restaurant. This provoked much debate about whether 'warehouse' was descriptive of a physical building or also of its permitted use. It was held to be descriptive only of the physical building and to mean a warehouse used for storage. However, the hypothetical warehouse could physically be used for retail and, given that the review clause contained a disregard of any restriction on use (which in any event allowed retail use with qualified consent (paras 9.3–9.10)), the prospect of obtaining a retail consent could be taken into account in valuation.

---

1   *Dukeminster (Ebbgate House One) Ltd v Somerfield Properties Co Ltd* (1997) 40 EG 157.
2   *Scottish Mutual Association Society v Secretary of State for the Environment* 1992 SLT 617, 1992 SCLR 247.
3   *McDonalds Real Estate LLP v Arundel Corp* [2008] EWHC 377(Ch).

8.33 Let in whole or in part. The tenant would prefer to obtain any quantum discount available and try to avoid a comparison with aggregated sub-rents. But, if the tenant has the right to sub-let in parts, that possibility would be reflected in the reviewed rent[1]. Sometimes parties agree to reflect contractually the absence or otherwise of sub-leases in existence at the review date.

---

1   *Lewisham Investment Partnership Ltd v Morgan* [1997] 51 EG 75.

8.34 Vacant Possession. To establish the market rent for the hypothetical lease requires the occupation of the actual tenant to be ignored but that simple, yet necessary, assumption of vacant possession has important consequences. In *99 Bishopsgate Ltd v Prudential Assurance Co Ltd*[1], it was held that the hypothetical tenant, faced with a very large vacant property assumed to be stripped of all tenant's fixtures and fittings[2], would negotiate a long rent-free period to enable it to find sub-tenants of part who themselves would require rent-free periods for fitting out. The actual tenant would, by contrast, pay the new rent from the review date with no rent-free period and consequently the rent at review was substantially discounted.

8.35 This was a worrying development for landlords because at that time rent-free periods were given to tenants at the start of a lease as compensation for the cost of fitting out and (in larger properties) also for the time and difficulty in sub-letting surplus parts. Initially they tackled the problem with an assumption that the premises were 'fit for immediate occupation and use' but difficulties of interpretation and resistance from tenants resulted. Tenants were concerned that the premises might be assumed to be free of all defects, even those for which they had no liability and further questions arose about the precise nature and standard of the assumed fitting-out works and the impact on rent. The concern of tenants that the phrase achieved more than the elimination of a rent-free period on review was matched by the worry of landlords that the phrase might fail to avoid the rent-free period[3].

8.36 In a climate where landlords and tenants generally agreed that rental concessions to the tenant should not be repeated at each review, landlords tackled the problem by drafting, referring specifically to such inducements. Notional rent-free periods or other rental concessions then commonly available on new lettings were to be disregarded but there were still difficulties of interpretation[4]. The commercial significance of such difficulties was greatly enhanced by market conditions in the 1990s which saw increasingly large one-off inducements (ie rent-free periods much longer than shopfitting periods and/or capital payments) being paid to tenants to 'compensate' them, not for the cost of fitting out, but for artificially high 'headline' rents. By arguing that rents which were artificially high due to support from substantial inducements should be used as comparables without downward adjustment, landlords were perceived as taking advantage of unexpected market conditions. Such was the opinion of Hoffmann J in *Co-operative Wholesale Society Ltd v National Westminster Bank plc*[5] who observed that this enabled the landlord to obtain a rent increase without any rise in property values or fall in the value of money and that 'in the absence of unambiguous language a court should not be ready to construe a rent review clause having this effect'. Of the four appeals heard together, only one succeeded. The same general approach was adopted here in *Church Commissioners for England and anor v Etam plc*[6] where it was held that the direction to disregard inducements required the valuer to adjust downwards comparable evidence where inducements had been given. Although the outcome was generally regarded as equitable, there is little certainty in the tortuous drafting which is part of the unreal world of rent review and landlords now generally appear to have settled for leases which prevent tenants from obtaining a rent reduction from the assumption of vacant possession.

8.37 Lastly, knowing that the assumption of vacant possession has the effect that sub-leases require to be ignored, parties if they wish otherwise should qualify appropriately the relevant assumption.

1   *99 Bishopsgate Ltd v Prudential Assurance Co Ltd* [1985] 1 EGLR 72.
2   *F R Evans (Leeds) Ltd v English Electric Co Ltd* (1977) 245 EG 657; [1978] 1 EGLR 93.
3   *Iceland Frozen Foods plc v Starlight Investment Ltd* [1992] 07 EG 117 but contrast *London and Leeds Estates Ltd v Paribas Ltd* [1993] 30 EG 89.
4   *City Offices plc v Bryanston Insurance Co Ltd* [1993] 1 EGLR 126.
5   *Co-operative Wholesale Society Ltd v National Westminster Bank plc* [1995] 1 EGLR 97 (heard with *Scottish Amicable Life Assurance Society v Middleton Potts & Co; Broadgate Square plc v Lehman Brothers Ltd* and *Prudential Nominees Ltd v Greenham Trading Ltd*).
6   *Church Commissioners for England and anor v Etam plc* 1997 SC 116, 1997 SLT 38.

8.38 Willing landlord/willing tenant. Such terms were considered in *F R Evans (Leeds) Ltd v English Electric Co Ltd*[1] and most leases direct that the existence of both be assumed. It has been held in England that the existence of a willing tenant is implied as being necessary to achieve an open market letting[2] but the genesis of that conclusion is the Landlord and Tenant Act 1954, s 34, which has no application in Scotland. If a tenant, having failed to find a purchaser of its interest despite extensive marketing, could satisfy the arbiter or expert that no one would take the hypothetical lease it seems unlikely that a Scottish court would allow the introduction of an assumption to the contrary. Landlords should therefore introduce the assumption of a willing tenant. It is unlikely that, given such poor market conditions, any uplift would result but such an assumption would prevent the rent plummeting if the lease contained no 'upward only' provision.

1   *F R Evans (Leeds) Ltd v English Electric Co Ltd* (1977) 245 EG 93.
2   *Dennis & Robinson Ltd v Kiossos Establishment* [1987] 1 EGLR 133.

8.39 Premium. To ensure that the rent is not distorted by capital payments which at the start of the hypothetical lease may be paid by either party to the other, the valuer should be directed to assume that no premiums are payable.

8.40 Duration. Although it is considered that, in the absence of any direction, the period of the actual lease unexpired at the relevant review date will be the assumed period of the hypothetical lease, the duration of the hypothetical lease is central to valuation and should be tackled by drafting which, to achieve its purpose, must be clear[1]. It is preferable to refer to a lease of a certain period of years to run from the relevant review date, rather than rely (as does the style in para 8.30) on a comparison with the duration of the original lease, the drafting of which can be open to more than one interpretation[2].

8.41 For many years it was argued that the level of rent on review increased with the duration of the assumed lease. The landlord argued for an assumed duration of 25 years; the tenant opted for the unexpired residue. Conventionally there was a compromise at 10 or 15 years, with the landlord's lawyer requiring a period sufficiently long to enable the hypothetical tenant to amortise any fitting-out expenditure. But the market is (and always was) more complicated than that. Although the general principle may have applied in a prime retail area (particularly if the property was on several floors and the review was to a 'shell', thereby increasing the cost of the hypothetical fitting out) it never had universal application to rents of warehouses or industrial units or some secondary retail pitches. Indeed with the advent of shorter leases of property of prime quality driven by the demands of tenants, it may be argued that the rent for an assumed longer duration would suffer a discount. Lawyers should ask for advice and not assume the continued applicability of the old ways in an ever-changing market.

8.42 A break clause (in favour of either or both parties) in the actual lease may be imported into the hypothetical lease of an assumed new duration by a reference to 'upon the terms and conditions contained herein' or similar phrase (para 8.43). That outcome depends on the drafting. In the absence of specific drafting on these points, it seems from the *St Martins* case (supra), that the hypothetical lease will not benefit from a break clause personal to the actual tenant nor when the actual lease identifies a precise option date that precedes the rent review date. The impact of break options on rent is highly material and it is preferable for careful drafting to put beyond doubt whether the break clause applies and, if so, when. Lawyers may need valuation advice as such a clause, including assumed duration provisions, can inflate or deflate rent depending on the market then applicable to the type of property concerned and the party or parties capable of exercising the option.

---

1 See *St Martin's Property Investments Ltd v CIB Properties Ltd* [1997] EGCS 99.
2 *Canary Wharf Investments (Three) v Telegraph Group Ltd* (2003) EHWC 1575 and *Monkspath Industrial Estate (No.1) Ltd and Anor v Lucas Industries Ltd* Unreported February 2006.

8.43 '... upon the terms and conditions (excluding rent) as are herein contained'. The valuer needs to know the terms of the hypothetical lease which are part of the comparison exercise. As a result of directions similar to those referred to in paragraphs 8.33, 8.34 and 8.40, the valuer has already been given instructions on several important areas and will require also to take into account the list of specific assumptions and disregards. The picture is completed by a requirement that the hypothetical lease be upon the terms and conditions of the actual lease. But in requiring the valuer to import into the hypothetical lease the general terms and conditions of the actual lease it is necessary to consider, firstly, an exclusion which was developed and which gave rise to considerable court intervention and, secondly, the consequences for the comparison exercise:

(i) Logically, one should exclude from the hypothetical lease the rent stated in the actual lease but a series of decisions in the English courts illuminated the dangers of using words which could extend that exclusion to the rent review itself. A hypothetical lease of an assumed duration of ten or more years would, in inflationary times, command a much higher rent, assuming no reviews (as opposed to the quinquennial review in the actual lease). Tenants who accepted an exclusion such as 'on the same terms and conditions (other than the amount of rent and the provisions of this clause for reviewing rent) as are contained in this lease ...' obtained no protection from the courts who found themselves unable to rewrite contracts whose terms, however unintentional, instructed the valuer to eliminate the review clause[1]. But then a single English judge in *National Westminster Bank Ltd v Arthur Young McLelland Moores & Co*[2] provoked fierce debate by holding that the words 'other than the rent hereby reserved' were in the context of the clause an instruction to disregard the review. Soon thereafter wiser counsel prevailed, concluding with *British Gas Corporation v Universities Superannuation Scheme*[3]. In these cases[4] the court opted to apply the underlying commercial purpose and to disregard the review clause only on very clear directions. Nevertheless, tenants should ensure that the drafting explicitly excludes any possibility of extension to other than the original rent in the actual lease.

(ii)   The comparison exercise inherent in rent review requires the valuer to adjust the rents otherwise derived from comparables to reflect the instructions in the rent review clause (para 8.27). If, by comparison with the leases of the comparable properties, the hypothetical lease is considered to have terms materially more onerous or more generous to the tenant, the hypothetical tenant would pay a different rent; the valuer's initial finding therefore requires upward or downward adjustment.

Against that background, the detailed terms of the actual lease (inserted into the hypothetical lease) can impact directly on the level of rent. Leases which contain restrictive clauses dealing with matters such as user[5], alienation, a joint and several obligation, alterations or keep open, when present singly or in combination, may result in a discount from the rent. In general terms the landlord has to balance control and income. In *Homebase Ltd v Scottish Provident Institution*[6] the court was asked to consider a lease which contained a normal Class 1 non-food user clause so that the landlord could not be accused of imposing unreasonable control to the extent that such restrictions may not apply to comparable leases. But the lease also contained a normal clause that required the tenant to comply with planning law and it transpired that an agreement under section 50 of the 1972 Planning Act (the modern equivalent of which is section 75 of the 1997 Planning Act as amended in 2006) restricted the use to a DIY store and garden centre. The court held that the restricted use was to be taken into account at review. Given that almost all leases will contain a clause that requires compliance by the tenant with a raft of statutory provisions including the Planning Acts (para 9.33) a landlord willing to loosen control by allowing a use wider than the then authorised planning use but in return expecting the rent on review to reflect that wider use would need the lease to contain a specific assumption of that use or, perhaps more suitably, a disregard of the restrictions of the planning regime (para 8.55). However, leaving aside any planning requirements, previous attempts to over-ride a restrictive user clause in the rent review provisions have generally met with considerable tenant resistance.

In support of the proposition that parties negotiating a lease should consider the overall impact of clauses it should be remembered that this comparison exercise between the terms of the hypothetical lease and the leases of the comparables can result in an addition to the rent to reflect a hypothetical lease more generous to the tenant than the comparables, such as where the tenant, alone in a shopping centre, is relieved of the responsibility of restoring latent defect damage.

1   See, eg *Pugh v Smith Industries* (1982) 264 EG 823 and *Safeway Food Stores Ltd v Banderway* (1983) 267 EG.
2   *National Westminster Bank Ltd v Arthur Young McLelland Moores & Co* [1985] 273 EG 402.
3   *British Gas Corporation v Universities Superannuation Scheme* [1986] 1 WLR 398.
4   See also *MFI Properties Ltd v BICC Group Pension Trust Ltd* [1986] 1 All ER 974.
5   *Plinth Property Investments Ltd v Mott, Hay and Anderson* (1979) 38 P&CR 361.
6   *Homebase Ltd v Scottish Provident Institution* 2004 SLT 296.

Specific Assumptions

8.44 As mentioned, these specific assumptions are intended to prevent a lowering of the rent due to the failings of the tenant or occupier but, as can be seen from the following consideration of those commonly appearing in leases, are often somewhat extended. These depend on individual circumstances but often include:

8.45

'... all of the obligations of the Landlord and the Tenant shall have been complied with (but without prejudice to any rights of either party in regard thereto)'.

The principle that a tenant should not benefit from its own breach is equitable and indeed the assumption of the tenant's compliance may be unnecessary as the hypothetical lease incorporates all of the tenant's obligations in the actual lease[1]. By contrast, the assumption of full compliance by the landlord seems to require the tenant to pay a level of rent based on something it does not have. In many leases where the landlord undertakes very few obligations (except insured risk damage – see para 8.48 and, possibly, damage by Uninsured Risks – see para 7.10) an argument on this matter is of academic interest. But in a multi-occupancy building (eg shopping centre or office block) the landlord is (or should be) under an obligation to maintain the whole structure, including common facilities, plant and equipment, and to provide a range of services (at the cost of the tenants). Tenants usually resist an assumption that such important and wide-ranging obligations have been fulfilled. Landlords counter that they should not be penalised when, at any particular review date, certain repair works happen then to be required. This assumption therefore provokes much discussion, but many tenants consider that major failures by the landlord will be reflected in the general 'tone' of the development and in the rents being achieved and in consequence will yield. A relatively common compromise is to assume performance by the landlord except where there is evidence of persistent material breach.

1   *Harmsworth Pension Funds Trustees Ltd v Charringtons Industrial Holdings Ltd* [1985] 1 EGLR 97.

8.46

'all parts of the Premises and the Common Parts are then ready fit and available for immediate use and occupation and could and would be immediately occupied by any willing tenant'.

This form of assumption is one of the consequences of the assumption of vacant possession but may be argued now to be unnecessary in dealing with rental concessions due to the emergence of more focused clauses on that subject (paras 8.34–8.37). Most tenants, concerned that it might have the effect of rentalising fitting-out works, will wish to simplify the assumption to that of the premises being ready for immediate occupation for fitting out.

8.47

'no work has been carried out to the Premises by the Tenant or any authorised occupier which has diminished the rental value thereof'.

Although a common assumption, it is questionable if it is legitimate. All works carried out by the tenant in terms of obligations of repair, decoration or compliance with statute, in the unlikely event of a potential for diminishing rental value, are assumed (para 8.45) to be carried out properly (ie in accordance with the tenant's obligations) and tenants should beware of being required to pay rent at a level which takes no account of work which is required by statute, for example creation of a fire corridor. All works voluntarily carried out by the tenant, whether or not considered as improvements, are likely to be the subject of a specific disregard (para 8.54).

8.48

'if the Premises and/or the Common Parts shall have been destroyed or damaged, the same shall have been fully reinstated as at the relevant rent review date'.

Tenants would generally accept that, for the purposes of rent review, damage by an insured risk should be assumed to have been restored. By its nature, insured risk damage is due to factors outwith the usual control of the parties, the timespan for restoration may be extensive and proper abatement provisions give the tenant protection. The same considerations extend to damage caused by one of the Uninsured Risks (para 7.10). However tenants are reluctant to see a blanket extension of this assumption to any other form of damage. Such damage could be caused, for example, by latent defect or even negligence or the deliberate act of the landlord. The precise extent to which the tenant has liability for any such damage will receive detailed attention elsewhere but, if within the responsibility of the tenant, it will be covered generally by the assumption considered in paragraph 8.45. It is difficult not to conclude that assuming the restoration of insured risk damage only is a reasonable middle course.

8.49

> 'the Tenant and the willing tenant are able to reclaim/recover in full all (if any) Value Added Tax chargeable on the rent and other monies payable by the Tenant'.

Most tenants pay VAT, so that VAT on the rent is confined to an administrative exercise. The two-tier market envisaged many years ago because of a substantial minority of tenants being VAT-adverse (eg financial institutions, some charities, medical organisations) has not materialised. Nevertheless, an assumption that the hypothetical tenant will recover VAT, or even, indeed, that the landlord should be assumed not to have elected (and be bound not to do so), is not uncommon. One could argue, however, that market forces can deal more flexibly with any such perceived problems and that the investigation of the calculation of all comparables (including the VAT element) is best left to informed judgment.

8.50 As mentioned at the beginning of paragraph 8.44, individual circumstances dictate the need for the range of required specific assumptions. Where the lease authorises a use for which any form of licence is needed, there should be an assumption that such a licence on normal terms is available.

Specific Disregards

8.51 As with assumptions, the original principle (in this case preventing rent increases due to the efforts or presence of the tenant) has been eroded over time by the inclusion of disregards intended to increase the rent. The list of disregards appearing in leases commonly includes:

8.52

> 'any effect on rent of the fact that the Tenant or any other authorised occupier may have been in occupation of the Subjects of Lease'.

This uncontentious disregard avoids the argument that a tenant in possession may pay more than the open market rent to avoid the disruption of leaving the property. A tenant also in occupation of neighbouring property would sensibly wish also to include it in the disregard to avoid any 'marriage value' discussion.

8.53

> 'any goodwill attached to the Subjects of Lease by reason of any trade or business carried on therein by the Tenant or any other authorised occupier'.

This too is uncontentious but tenants in appropriate circumstances should ensure that the drafting encompasses all predecessors in the relevant business including those whose occupation pre-dates the lease.

8.54 *'Improvements.'* It is widely regarded as unfair to require a tenant to pay any additional rent attributable to its own improvements to the property. However the application of the maxim *'inaedifactum solo, solo cedit'* produces that result[1]. The ownership having been settled in favour of the landlord, the tenant (particularly in a ground lease) must ensure that the lease contains clear directions to disregard improvements at review[2] The absence from this text of any introductory words illustrative of a commonly framed disregard is testament to the drafting difficulties which have emerged and been tested in court. The two principal issues to be considered are the nature of the works to be disregarded and the valuation consequences:

    (i)   A consideration of the nature of the 'improvements' brings these points into play in adjusting a suitable clause:

        •   Although this disregard is generally intended to avoid a tenant being rentalised on its own capital expenditure (or 'improvements'), works done to suit a tenant's personal needs may diminish rental value. By the use of words such as 'any effect on rent of any works', the rent is adjusted, upwards or downwards, to reflect the impact of the works. Tenants find difficulty in resisting this point (although the rent review implications of voluntary works are likely to be reflected in any licence for works) but should bear in mind that they would obtain no reduction in rent where works were undertaken in implementation of a statutory obligation. (see also sub para (b) below)

- Any improvements carried out by a tenant which precede the date of entry will be excluded from the disregard and some leases so state specifically. Tenants should qualify appropriately where work is started before that date for any reason (and the use of 'access dates' is common – see paras 2.13–2.17) or where the tenant is taking a new lease on expiry of a previous right of occupancy during which improvements were made.

- It is submitted that this disregard should come into operation except to the extent that the landlord has paid for the works. But tenants should guard against improvements qualifying only if 'carried out by the Tenant at its own cost' or something similar. Words like 'free of cost to the Landlord' are helpful.

- Phrases such as 'otherwise than in pursuance of any obligation to the Landlord' comprise a common unexceptional exclusion from this disregard. However, tenants often inherit a 'developer's shell' requiring considerable expenditure, the range of documents which may contain an obligation to the landlord increases, a landlord may be offering financial incentives to assist with fitting-out works and tenants often take access before the date of entry. All these developments require that both parties be very clear about this exclusion and the following should be borne in mind:

(a) The tenant may consider adding 'herein contained' with the aim of avoiding the inclusion of obligations in deeds such as the agreement for lease, a fitting-out licence or a licence for alterations, albeit that in the latter case the English courts have tended to interpret any obligation as being limited to the method of executing the works[3]. A landlord disposed to accept such a revisal should consider whether all fitting-out works should be ignored at review, document where the landlord may be contributing financially and have regard to the assumed duration of the hypothetical lease. In the latter context, a landlord may be faced at year 20 of a 25-year lease with a property on several floors handed over to a tenant as a shell lacking inter alia lifts, stairs and escalators being rentalised on the hypothesis of a lease duration too short to amortise the incoming hypothetical tenant's necessary fitting-out works. Sometimes parties agree an assumption of certain basic fitting-out works.

(b) The lease will contain an obligation on the tenant to comply with statute and tenants will wish to agree drafting which disregards such works.

(c) It is reasonable for landlords to limit the disregard of improvements to those for which the tenant has been granted consent. Although such works are usually likely to be of little valuation significance (but could be in a ground lease) tenants may wish to add 'if required', particularly in the light of the English decision in *Hamish Cathie Travel England Ltd v Insight International Tours Ltd*[4].

(ii) The valuation consequences of a disregard of improvements were considered in *GREA Real Property Investments Ltd v Williams*[5], from which the following themes emerged:

- The intention of the parties (unless clear drafting states otherwise) is to enable the landlord to obtain at review any increase in rental value not attributable to improvements made by the tenant.

- Provided that the valuer properly reflects those intentions, the choice of valuation method is not a question of law.

- There are advantages in the use, where available, of comparables of property in an unimproved state.

- In the absence of comparables of unimproved properties, the choice of method remains that of the valuer.

Such general propositions will apply whether the lease directs that the improvements or their effect on rent be disregarded.

---

1   *Brand's Trustees v Brands Trustees* (1876) 3 R (HL) 16 and *Shetlands Islands Council v BP Petroleum Development Ltd* 1990 SLT 82.

2   For cases where difficulties of interpretation arose (with different results), see *Ponsford v HMS Aerosols Ltd* [1979] AC 63; *Ipswich Town Football Club v Ipswich Borough Council* (1988) EG 49; *PIK Facilities Ltd v Lord Advocate* 1997 SCLR 855.

3   *Godbold v Martin the Newsagents Ltd* (1983) 268 EG 1202. But see *Ivory Gate Ltd v Capital City Leisure Ltd* [1993] EGCS 76.

4   *Hamish Cathie Travel England Ltd v Insights International Tours Ltd* [1986] 1 EGLR 244.

5   *GREA Real Property Investments Ltd v Williams* (1979) 250 EG 651.

8.55 Certain disregards are intended to increase the rent, not (as with the previous three) to avoid increases.

The objective requires that the tenant considers any such disregards very carefully. Common examples are:

- A tight user restriction. As previously mentioned (para 8.43), by the use of an assumption or disregard, the landlord can combine control and income to the obvious disadvantage of the tenant.

- Statutory restrictions (eg conditions or limitations) in a planning permission. The disregard of a condition on a planning permission which, for example, limits the proportion of floor area devoted to retail or restricts the range of goods to be sold might materially increase the rent to be paid by the tenant itself prevented from so trading.

- The need to tackle the rent review consequences of rental concessions was raised earlier (para 8.36) in the context of the necessary assumption of vacant possession. Landlords should ensure that the valuer is directed to disregard the absence of such concessions or inducements and tenants should resist any drafting which extends beyond the inducements related to fitting out.

- The inability of the tenant to recover VAT in full. This is a rehearsal of the equivalent assumption (para 8.49).

The Comparison Exercise

8.56 This requires the valuer to obtain evidence of lettings of properties comparable to the subjects of lease carried out on comparable terms. We have already seen (para 8.43) the importance of the lease terms in the exercise but, nevertheless, the end result remains a matter of informed judgment, not an exact science, particularly where there are no direct comparables and much adjustment to individual components is necessary. Sometimes the absence of comparables can be anticipated when the lease is negotiated (para 8.32) because the property and/or its location may be highly unusual in which event the rent may be geared to some other set of circumstances capable of ready ascertainment.

8.57 Gearing provisions, while sometimes necessary (and common in ground leases of undeveloped land), can have unpredictable consequences and must be very carefully drafted in co-operation with surveyors[1]. Even relatively simple provisions supported by worked examples can cause disputes[2].

8.58 The relevant date for assessment of the new rent is usually the rent review date but frequently the independent third party hears evidence from parties much later than that. The question then arises as to the admissibility of evidence which came into existence after the rent review date. The question appears to have been settled in England following the *Segama NV v Penny Le Roy Ltd* case[3] where evidence of open market lettings and rent review agreements dated after the review date was admitted.

---

1   See *Equity & Law life Assurance Society plc v Bodfield Ltd* [1987] 281 EG 1448 and *British Railways Board v Ringbest* [1996] 30 EG 94 for unexpected results.
2   *City Wall Properties (Scotland) Ltd v Pearl Assurance plc* [2007] CSIH 79; *Nissim v Ablethird* [2009] EWHC 585 (Ch).
3   *Segama NV v Penny Le Roy Ltd* (1983) 269 EG 322.

THIRD PARTY DETERMINATION

General

8.59 In the event that the parties cannot agree upon the rent to apply after review, there must be a mechanism for determination of the rent by reference to a third party otherwise the review clause will be void from uncertainty[1]. The identity of the third party, failing agreement between the parties, is usually settled by the Chairman (and failing him, the Vice-Chairman) of the Scottish Branch of the Royal Institution of Chartered Surveyors. Provision should be made for a replacement should the original appointment fail.

---

1   *Beard v Beveridge, Herd & Sandilands* 1990 SLT 609. See also *Crawford v Bruce* 1992 SLT 524 and for a different result *City of Aberdeen Council v Clark* 1999 SLT 613.

Timing of Appointment

8.60 The valuation date is usually the rent review date. Therefore a reference to the third party months earlier is unlikely to advance matters. Conversely, a delayed reference has some dangers. The tenant may be paying a penalty interest rate on undetermined rent (para 8.65) and will not have budget certainty for its business or for any sale of its interest.

The landlord would have reservations about a tenant (other than a very powerful one) building up a considerable shortfall in rent payments. Of course, depending upon the rental market, either landlord or tenant may want a delay to introduce post-review date evidence. Generally, however, both parties prefer certainty.

At one time it was common for landlords to fix provisional rents to apply while the new rent was being determined. However, tenants resisted paying an interim rent based on an estimate by the landlord of the likely new rent. Complications arose about rates of interest on sums overpaid and generally the procedure seems to have disappeared from most leases now being granted.

For that reason, most rent review clauses now proceed on the basis that either party can trigger the appointment of the third party at any time after a specified date (usually the rent review date).

Experience and Status of Third Party

8.61 A frequent complaint of landlords and tenants is that of inadequate experience of the independent valuer appointed to fix the new rent. Accordingly it has become common for rent review clauses to set down criteria about the length of required experience.

Of more difficulty is the question of whether the valuer should be an arbiter or an expert. It is suggested that those adjusting leases should have regard to the following:

- A provision entitling one party (usually the landlord) to choose the status of the valuer for any particular review is manifestly unfair.

- Most leases provide for the expert a series of detailed instructions which greatly exceed that of requiring the valuer to decide on an appropriate rent. In consequence, most 'experts' are constrained by their terms of reference but that does not convert an expert into an arbiter[1].

- The benefits claimed for determination by an expert are speed and reduced cost. Where the issues are likely to be relatively simple and there will be no absence of comparables, this method may commend itself to parties.

- A challenge to the arbiter's final award could be on only very limited grounds[3].

- Unless otherwise required by the lease, the expert can disregard all representations and rely on his own expertise, subject to his contingent liability for negligence. That said, the valuer would be liable only if his performance would fall short of that expected of a surveyor of usual competence practising in the rent review field[2]. That said, although it was generally thought that an expert's decision could not be appealed except on a ground such as corruption, in England[4] the courts may now accept that an expert's decision may be reviewable if he has misinterpreted the legal effect of a rent review clause.

- An expert has no power to award fees or expenses or to have these taxed so the lease must give him that power; in contrast, an arbiter has full discretion.

- The general view is that, the more complicated the circumstances, arbitration becomes the safer option.

---

1   *AGE Ltd v Kwik-Save Stores Ltd* 2001 SLT 841; *Holland House Property Investments Ltd v Crabbe* 2008 SC 619.
2   *Lewisham v Morgan* [1997] 51 EG 75.
3   *West v Secretary of State for Scotland* 1992 SLT 636.
4   *National Grid Co plc v M25 Group Ltd* [1999] EGCS 2.

Cases Presented to Third Party

8.62 The exercise carried out by the valuers for the landlord and the tenant and the presentation of such cases to the third party, whether orally or in writing, is outwith the scope of this work but two matters are worthy of brief mention. Rent review surveyors have faced criticism in the English courts when presenting evidence in rent review arbitrations. The consequence is that present guidance to the surveying profession[1] suggests that they must define their role clearly but provided they do so they may act either as an expert or surveyor advocate or even in a dual role in the same case. Although this publication, including its appendix containing extracts on the guidance notes for surveyors when acting as experts, does clearly explain the difficulties and requirements in these various circumstances, one problem which has recently occurred is the role of the surveyor advocate. There is a body of opinion in both the surveying and legal professions that a surveyor advocate acting solely in that capacity is immune from cross-examination. This could cause difficulties at a hearing where valuation evidence for the other party is given by a surveyor acting as an expert susceptible to cross-examination and, perhaps unsurprisingly, a contrary view that a surveyor advocate can be compelled to give evidence has also been expressed. It would be surprising if this matter did not resurface. The dual role issue may also have some relevant to 'Calderbank' offers, named after an English case in 1975[2]. This is a procedure used by rent review surveyors, similar to a tender in court, by which a party makes a written offer to settle a review at a specified figure (usually with each party paying its own legal expenses plus half of the arbiter's fee) and stating that it is without prejudice except as to expenses, usually leading to the arbiter awarding expenses to the successful party. In the context of the dual role of rent review surveyors, is it legitimate for an expert witness to argue for a rent higher than that in his Calderbank letter?

---

1 Surveyors acting as advocates, RICS practice statement and guidance note (GN 2nd edition, combined PS and GN 1st edition) January 2009.

2 *Calderbank v Calderbank* [1975] 3 All ER 333 and *Cutts v Head* [1984] Ch 290.

PROCEDURAL MATTERS

8.63 The fourth element in rent review clauses (after implementing the review, defining the open market rent and providing for third party determination in a dispute) comprises procedural matters:

Rent payments

8.64 Rarely is the new rent known by the review date. Unless the lease provides for the fixing of a provisional rent (para 8.60), it will require the tenant to pay rent at the old rate on account of the new rent until ascertained.

Shortfall/Interest

8.65 On the new rent being determined, the lease will provide a date (usually 14 days or so after ascertainment) within which the tenant must pay the shortfall. It is accepted that the landlord should receive interest on this shortfall but the following points should be considered when adjusting the clause.

- The tenant should ensure that interest runs on each component part of the shortfall, not on the total, where more than one rent payment date has passed, otherwise the landlord is overcompensated[1].

- The rate of interest should be reduced from the penalty rate to a rate which gives neither party an incentive to delay the review.

- The landlord, in agreeing the lower rate of interest, should preserve the right to penalty interest if payment of the shortfall plus interest is itself delayed.

---

1   *Bradford & Bingley Building Society v Thorntons plc* 1998 GWD 40–2071.

Counter-inflation Legislation

8.66 Although long since repealed, landlords remember when the collection of increases in rent of business premises was statutorily restricted and they still draw clauses intended to introduce intermediate review dates when any such legislation (if enacted) would allow. But various problems emerge as any such government interference inevitably distorts the market. For the review to take place despite the legislation and for the uplift to arise to the extent that statute allows (which was the effect of the 1973 legislation) carries the difficulty of a possible lack of rental evidence due to a limited number of reviews being effected. To allow the introduction of an interim review date in substitution for the original planned review date might mean a severe increase caused by unfulfilled demand. Given that a repeat of such legislation is generally regarded as very unlikely, parties are usually able to reach agreement, often by a provision that the reviewed rent will not exceed that which would apply in the absence of the legislation, albeit that such a determination is itself not free from difficulty.

Rent Review Memoranda

8.67 For sensible management reasons, parties should execute a memorandum of the rent after review, even if some landlords are reluctant when no increase has resulted. The availability of a memorandum may also help the landlord in the recovery of arrears if it contains a clause of consent to registration for preservation and execution. In the event of a dispute about the level of agreed rent, in the absence of a memorandum one could turn to informal correspondence. In this respect it is likely that such letters as were written on a 'without prejudice' basis would be deprived of any protection after agreement had been reached.

ALTERNATIVE RENT REVIEW PROCEDURES

8.68 Increasing dissatisfaction with the expensive, time-consuming and adversarial process which comprises the type of rent review previously described in this chapter has led parties to consider alternative options. Avoiding reviews completely by leases of five years or less is usually impractical where, despite current trends, the requirement of the landlord for a guaranteed income for a longer period is matched by that of the tenant for security of tenure for a period sufficiently long to amortise expenditure on improvements. Leases for, say, ten years at an annual rent exceeding by an agreed percentage the open market rent at entry are a gamble for both parties. However, there are the following alternatives to the usual rent review method although, as will be seen, the reason for the last is dictated not by considerations of simplicity but by commercial reasons.

Index-linked Rents

8.69 This is a simple and certain method of reviewing the rent at any agreed interval because an accurately drafted clause will provide an arithmetically sound answer. However, that certainty comes at the price of the absence of any link between the reviewed rent and the intervening changes in the value of property and money, for these reasons:

8.70 The absence of an index based on property values or rental levels, even at a national level; in any event, national figures bear little relationship to regional, let alone local, conditions.

8.71 The rent that a particular property could command, if offered on the market, may be affected by circumstances, such as the opening of a new shopping centre, which are peculiar to a very localised area.

8.72 Any index is susceptible to being re-based or disappearing and in either case, to prevent failure of the review clause, a reference to a third party determining a substitute index will be required.

The reality is that indexation merely results in a rent being increased (assuming that the drafting excludes a decrease) in line with the general form of inflation that exists in the sectors that fall within the index. The rent thus calculated bears no necessary relationship to that which tenants are paying in the marketplace for similar property taken on similar leases. A landlord may therefore be losing substantial income, or a tenant may be paying substantially more than the open market rent and encounter difficulties in assigning.

Stepped Rents

8.73 Total certainty on future rents is guaranteed by agreeing specific increases at identified future dates and such a procedure is now regularly used. Tolerances linking to an index sometimes appear and some clauses maintain a link to property by setting rent as the lower of the open market rent and a stated percentage increase.

Turnover Rents

8.74 Turnover rents imply a degree of partnership between landlord and tenant, with the former obtaining an income based on the turnover of the business being conducted from the subjects of lease. To that extent, therefore, they may represent a movement back from the adversarial approach that inhabits many elements of the conventional lease, including rent reviews. However, although some leases are structured in this way, turnover rents remain relatively unpopular, for the following reasons:

8.75 Not all commercial properties create a turnover capable of being measured. Shops, public houses or food courts are obvious candidates but properties such as warehousing or distribution centres or administrative offices do not provide turnover figures.

8.76 Rarely will a landlord wish to link its income exclusively to turnover figures, thereby substituting for a market-led rent an income at the mercy of fluctuating figures unrelated to property. That said it is not unknown for a landlord, anxious to tempt into a new shopping centre prospective tenants expressing reluctance due to concerns about trading prospects, to offer a turnover rent agreement personal to that tenant. Such an agreement would replace the lease rental provisions with the turnover clause but only until a completed assignation or sub-letting or, if earlier, the date on which the tenant ceased trading from the whole of the property. It follows that the rent must still be reviewed in the conventional way so as to be available for immediate implementation in any of the events described. Usually, however, the landlord wants the comfort of support for the turnover rent and that can be achieved in several ways. A base rent of an agreed amount is a simple method of providing a minimum return although, with inflation, over time the level of support is reduced. More commonly, turnover rent leases preserve a normal rent review clause as a base or fallback, requiring payment by the tenant of an agreed percentage (commonly 80%) of the open market rent as reviewed and with the landlord 'topping-up' its income from the turnover provisions. Ironically therefore, such turnover rent provisions do not eradicate the complex rent review clauses that they are designed to replace.

8.77 Indeed, turnover rent provisions are themselves somewhat complicated, as to both the components of turnover and the timing consequences, and the solicitors for both parties should rely heavily on the advice of the clients' accountants. From the landlord's perspective, turnover figures should include, in the case of retail, all sales, services or supplies from the premises generated by orders of any nature, including the internet, and for the full cash price irrespective of the means of payment. Among concerns of the tenant would be exclusions of uncollectable accounts. Provision for determination by a turnover specialist of any dispute is relatively common. By its very nature, a turnover rent cannot be calculated in advance so provision has to be made for payments based on the preceding year's figures (or on the base rent in the first year) with subsequent adjustment. The landlord should ensure that the tenant is obliged to produce proper records and allow inspection.

Affordability Models

8.78 The last alternative to the usual rent review method differs from the other two in that the objective is not avoidance of the complexities of regular rent reviews based on open market value. Instead it is argued that one can more accurately measure what the willing tenant would pay in rent, particularly for a foodstore, by the use of an 'affordability' model than by the use of comparables in the conventional way. The model adopts similar criteria to those applied by retailers evaluating the viability of a projected store, including the competition in the catchment area, and concludes with an 'affordable rent'. Such an argument has been used with some success at arbitrations as a component in the general argument. Nevertheless this procedure does not appear to be much used.

Green issues

8.79 The extent to which green leases are used and developed may to some extent depend on the impact of green provisions on rent and its review. Such leases, if containing very onerous terms, or subject in practice to unusually large CRC costs or perceived inequities in calculation, may result in tenants arguing for discounts. On specifics, a green lease might contain the following matters additional to the norm:

- An assumption that the property has an EPC whose recommendations have been implemented;

- An explicit inclusion of green improvements in the disregard applying to those carried out free of expense to the landlord (para 8.54).

Chapter 9

The Tenant's General Obligations

CONTROL

9.1 Those obligations (financial or money-related) flowing from the concept of a full repairing and insuring lease with rent reviews are considered in Chapter 4 with reference to individual chapters on repairs, service charge, insurance and rent review. The general obligations usually imposed on the tenant are, with the exception of alienation, intended broadly to control its activities while in occupation. These controls, particularly in an enclosed development, can be extremely detailed and to an extent governed by the precise nature of that development. What follows are the more important elements likely to be of importance to the parties in most commercial leases. The control over the activities of the tenant which the landlord wishes to enforce can be:

- absolute;
- subject to consent;
- subject to qualified consent.

9.2 Absolute control is needed in certain circumstances. For example, the landlord must avoid the tenant using the subjects of lease for a purpose unauthorised by the Planning Acts or conducting operations that might jeopardise the structural integrity of the property or in such a way as would breach another tenant's exclusivity clause. Nevertheless, absolute control resting with the landlord should generally be resisted by the tenant and viewed with caution by the landlord in case it triggers a discount at rent review (para 8.43 (ii)). The tenant's solicitor may choose to fetter control by the addition of 'without the consent of the landlord'. But Scots law contains no implication that consent is not to be unreasonably withheld[1] nor does the Law of Property Act 1925 (which in the context of assignation implies that consent will not be unreasonably withheld)' apply here. Despite obiter comments in one English case[2], it is highly unlikely that such a phrase would reduce the potential for a discount at rent review. The normal method of diluting absolute control is by reference to consent that is 'not to be unreasonably withheld' ie qualified consent.

---

1   *Muir v Wilson* 20 January 1820 FC 83.
2   *Forte & Co Ltd v General Accident Life Assurance Ltd* [1986] 2 EGLR 115.

QUALIFIED CONSENT

9.3 The expression 'such consent not to be unreasonably withheld' became common in commercial leases on the arrival of English institutions anxious to invest in Scottish property and armed with instructions to their newly acquired Scottish solicitors to draw leases to the same effect as though the property were in England. Given that, conceptually, the Scottish lease is a contract whereas the English equivalent is an estate in land, this grafting of English objectives on to our system created difficulties. For example, in the application of qualified consent to alienation one had first to overcome the tenant's implied right to assign or sub-let (para 4.3), then control the details of alienation by contractual provisions, including limiting absolute control by reference to consent not to be unreasonably withheld. And as we see in paragraph 9.14, further considerations are applied to alienation.

9.4 Advising clients, particularly on vital matters like alienation, was not assisted by an absence of judicial authority. Some practitioners considered that refusal of consent where the prospective tenant could be shown to be capable of performing the tenant's obligations was 'unreasonable'. Others, probably in the majority, thought that consent could reasonably be refused provided that the landlord had not acted merely capriciously or perversely. Meantime, in England, cases such as *Bromley Park Gardens Estates Ltd v Moss*[1] and *International Drilling Fluids Ltd v Louisville Investments (Uxbridge) Ltd*[2] showed that, certainly in that country, a landlord could not legitimately refuse consent for a collateral purpose and that the interests of the tenant also merited consideration. Then in 1988 the Inner House in *Renfrew District Council v AB Leisure (Renfrew) Ltd (in liqn)*[3] considered an alienation clause excluding assignees 'except with the consent in writing of the landlord which consent shall not be unreasonably withheld and shall not be withheld where the resources of the assignees are adequate to carry out this lease'.

9.5 The landlord consented subject to four conditions. The tenant's liquidator accepted the first condition requiring payment of rent arrears. The other three conditions were directed towards materially changing the terms of the lease to the landlord's advantage. Upholding the decision of the sheriff (who had found the English decisions helpful), the court decided that conditions divorced from the terms of the existing lease were unreasonable and their imposition equated to an unreasonable withholding of consent. In *Lousada & Co Ltd v J E Lesser (Properties) Ltd*[4], perhaps surprisingly, the court held that the landlord was entitled to impose a condition requiring settlement of a rent review because this was not a collateral benefit.

---

1   *Bromley Park Gardens Estates Ltd v Moss* [1982] 2 All ER 890.
2   *International Drilling Fluids Ltd v Louisville Investments Uxbridge Ltd* [1986] 1 All ER 321.
3   *Renfrew District Council v AB Leisure (Renfrew) Ltd (in liqn)* 1988 SCLR 512, 1988 SLT (Notes) 635 (IH).
4   *Lousada & Co Ltd v J E Lesser (Properties) Ltd* 1990 SC 178, 1990 SLT 823.

9.6 Over time, following cases such as those involving Tesco[1] and Burger King[2] the principles are now established as:

- The onus of showing that consent has been unreasonably withheld, unlike in England, lies with the tenant.

- Consent cannot be refused for a collateral purpose, a matter to be judged from the lease terms and the intention of the parties at the outset.

- The decision is based on the conclusion of a reasonable landlord irrespective of whether the court would have reached that decision.

- The general rule that the landlord need consider only its own interests is modified where the detriment to the tenant of refusal significantly outweighs the disadvantages to the landlord.

- Only the landlord's state of knowledge and reasons for refusal at the decision point are relevant, and

- Whether the landlord has unreasonably refused consent is, subject to these principles, a matter of fact.

9.7 Indeed the circumstances at play in each case can vary considerably and can relate to matters other than alienation on which, understandably, there has been the most focus. To those requiring to give advice when facing such a dispute, often involving pressing commercial concerns such as the impending disappearance of a prospective assignee, judging the likely outcome may not be easy. Is a landlord obliged to consent to an application from a nationally represented retailer to assign to an established and profitable local trader the lease of a shop in a country town where its experienced valuation surveyor considers that the capital value of the landlord's small development comprising a few units would be materially and adversely affected while conceding that few national retailers have a presence in that town. Is a landlord having an established ethical posture entitled to refuse consent to an assignation to a substantial retailer operating on the margins of the sex industry where the authorised user clause requires no alteration? Moving from alienation, can a landlord refuse a change of use to one of which it is known to disapprove on moral grounds? Indeed, alienation and user are closely linked with landlords sometimes trying to refuse consent to assign because of concerns regarding user. In *Ashworth Frazer v Gloucester City Council*[3] the House of Lords in an English appeal refused to elevate to a principle the idea that the landlord's reasonably held belief that a proposed assignee would breach the user clause was a ground for refusal, as that position could sometimes be unreasonable, a position adopted by the Scottish courts in *Scottish Property Investment Ltd v Scottish Provident Ltd*[4]. It is worth noting that in England, it has been held that a landlord requires not only to advance a reason for refusal of consent which is reasonable, but that the court may want to scrutinise the advice on which the refusal is based[5], and in Scotland it has been held that a landlord with a legitimate reason for refusal (eg covenant) cannot impose a premium on its grant of consent[6].

---

1   *Legal & General Assurance Society v Tesco Stores Ltd,* OH, Lord Hamilton, unreported (2001 GWD 18–707).

2   *Burger King Ltd v Rachel Charitable Trust Ltd* 2006 SLT 224.
3   *Ashworth Frazer v Gloucester City Council* [2001] PLSCS 223.
4   *Scottish Property Investment Ltd v Scottish Provident Ltd* 2004 GWD 6–120.
5   *Luminar Leisure Ltd v Apostole* 42 EG 140.
6   *Scottish Tourist Board v Deanpark Ltd* 1998 SLT (Sh Ct) 1121.

9.8 *Renfrew District Council v AB Leisure (Renfrew) Ltd (in liqn)* also decided that the usual remedy for a tenant where the landlord unreasonably withheld consent was an action in damages for breach of contract, not (as in England) a declarator. Furthermore, from remarks made obiter in *Scotmore Developments v Anderton*[1], it seems likely that an unjustified refusal to grant consent is a material breach going to the root of the contract and entitling the tenant to rescind.

1   *Scotmore Developments Ltd v Anderton* 1996 SC 368, 1996 SLT 1304.

9.9 There has been much debate on the need to add to the normal phrase words such as 'or delayed' or 'or a decision thereon unreasonably delayed'. The need for any such additional words is extremely doubtful but an anxious tenant's solicitor could include this as part of the interpretation clause, thereby avoiding lengthy repetitive drafting on each of the many occasions in a lease where qualified consent is mentioned.

9.10 A landlord may want the right automatically to refuse consent if the consent of a superior landlord or heritable creditor cannot be obtained. The tenant should insist that the basis for consent from the landlord should be unaffected by the actions of such a third party whose rights to refuse consent would need to be judged on the basis of the terms of the head lease or standard security involved.

ALIENATION

9.11 As discussed in paragraph 4.3, the landlord must exclude by express drafting the common law right of the tenant to assign or sub-let without consent, particularly given the usual absence of any recourse post-assignation against the original tenant. In a consideration of the detailed alienation provisions (unless the duration is very short) parties should expect that the tenant may wish at some point to dispose of the property. If the controls fixed by the landlord are absolute or even unusually demanding, the lease may be unmarketable, leaving the tenant unable to offer it as security and remaining liable for rent and the other obligations after its need for the property has ceased. Because an unmarketable lease would impact adversely on the rent at review, it is equally in the interests of the landlord to adjust an alienation clause which provides for both parties a reasonable measure of flexibility. The usual components of a modern alienation clause are:

9.12 A prohibition against any dealing (by which is meant an assignation, sub-lease, charging or a parting or sharing of possession) in part of the subjects of lease. Given obvious management problems with separate leases of parts of the original subjects of lease, tenants can accept this principle but by reference to a phrase such as 'except as may be expressly hereinafter provided' exclude from the ambit of the prohibition certain types of occupation of retail subjects (para 9.20) and limited sub-leases (para 9.15).

9.13 A prohibition against any dealing in the whole subjects of lease except by an assignation, sub-let or charge allowed under subsequent provisions. As in paragraph 9.12, the tenant may wish to exclude other specifically allowed occupational rights.

9.14 A prohibition against assignations, sub-leases or the granting of securities over the whole save with consent not to be unreasonably withheld. This brings into play the various factors discussed at length in paragraphs 9.3–9.10. Additionally, however, the following elements may feature:

- the landlord may require the assignee, sub-tenant etc to be 'respectable and responsible, of sound financial standing and demonstrably capable of fulfilling the obligations of the tenant under this lease or the intended sub-lease' or some variation thereof. The addition of such qualities is reasonable but, in combination with other elements of this clause tends to 'provide practice in mental acrobatics on the high wire of the multiple negative', as one unnamed commentator observed[1], a comment that remains pertinent more than 35 years later. The strict interpretation of many alienation provisions so qualified gives the landlord absolute control where all the criteria are not met and does not fetter the landlord's right to withhold consent reasonably even if these qualities are present. The different terminology in the case of *Renfrew District Council v AB Leisure (Renfrew) Ltd*[2] should be noted;

- in the case of a private limited company, the consent may be stated to allow the landlord in its absolute discretion to require a guarantor who must execute a guarantee in the form of the annexed draft (para 4.8). A well-advised tenant would argue that the need for a guarantor should be assessed against the qualified controls already discussed;

- clauses requiring the tenant to obtain a direct obligation from the assignee; these are unnecessary in Scotland;

- the landlord may require a tenant seeking consent to dispose of its lease to offer to renounce. This is attractive to landlords in modern shopping centres, concerned to maximise control over tenant mix. Provided that the clause is expressed as a pre-emption so that the tenant obtains market value (which would include goodwill, if relevant), one of the major concerns is allayed. However, tenants prefer to avoid the clause because of difficulties in marketing a property known to be subject to a pre-emption right and to possible difficulties when the tenant is marketing a portfolio of properties. Concerns that the Conveyancing Amendment (Scotland) Act 1938, s 9 (as amended) would limit the pre-emption right to one operation are often addressed by each assignee being required to grant an undertaking to the landlord;

- a request by a tenant to be entitled to assign without consent to any related company of the tenant should be resisted. Sharing or parting with occupation to a related company is considered in paragraph 9.20.

---

1   1976 JLSS p436.
2   1988 SCLR 512, 1988 SLT (Notes) 635 (IH).

9.15 Controls over sub-leases are usually imposed. By way of introduction, it should be realised that some landlords try to prevent sub-leases of the whole, let alone part. This may stem from a wish to avoid the tenant realising a profit rental (and may explain also the attempts by some landlords to share the premium on an assignation as a condition of the grant of consent). Rarely would a tenant accept a bar on a sub-lease of the whole, partly because this may be the only practical disposal route if the potential tenant is unacceptable to the landlord due to issues of covenant. There is some justification for prohibiting or limiting sub-leases of part, not due to the erroneous belief that, as in England, the failure of the head lease would leave sub-leases in place, but because fragmentation of occupation should be avoided. Where (and only where) a property can be physically sub-divided to provide more than one unit of decent accommodation, sub-leases of a limited number and identified size tolerances should be considered. The tenant of a whole office block would expect the right to sub-let single (but whole) floors.

9.16 However, presuming that the landlord accepts that the tenant may grant a sub-lease (or sub-leases) the preference of the landlord is that all sub-leases should:

- command a rent not less than the higher of the open market rent (which may be a defined term and be subject to the upward-only principle) and the passing rent. This is designed to preserve good rental evidence for the whole development.

- contain obligations on the part of the sub-tenant in the same form as those of the tenant.

9.17 These two controls cause problems, principally because tenants need to anticipate a future depressed market, such that only by reducing the rent below the passing rent and/or by diluting the obligations of the sub-tenant (for example, on repairs) could the tenant hope to dispose of its lease. The response of the well advised tenant is to argue that in respect of the first point the lease should provide for any sub-lease to be granted at no less than the then current open market rent, although one has to be careful with definitions and agreement on that rent has the propensity to delay the grant of consent. On the second point it is difficult for the lease to set forth a regime that would allow a dilution of landlord control in a range of possible future circumstances and, despite the concerns of the tenant, the clause is often left unqualified with tenants hoping that landlords will be amenable to compromise if difficult market conditions exist when the sub-lease is being negotiated.

9.18 If the tenant is contemplating a sub-lease out of a lease with these controls particularly on rent, the temptation exists to produce for the landlord's approval a sub-lease which meets the required criteria but to enter into a private arrangement with the sub-tenant. These issues were debated in a comparatively recent English case[1] in the Court of Appeal where it was held that the sub-lease and side letter were interdependent; there were clear rental and repairs implications for the landlord and the landlord was entitled to refuse consent. Some of the arguments involved technical points of English law but it seems very likely that the same result would have ensued in a similar Scottish case. If the tenant keeps the landlord unaware of these personal terms, the danger of a subsequent action of irritancy is clear. Whether the landlord in the then prevailing circumstances would wish so to proceed is a matter of judgment but the sub-tenant's position would be perilous, even though the tenant might be content to be relieved of a problem property. It would be possible for the tenant to provide to the sub-tenant a form of indemnity from a third party (for practical purposes likely to be connected to the tenant) but that would not dilute the sub-lease obligations[2]. It would however reduce the exposure of the sub-tenant.

1   *Allied Dunbar Assurance plc v Homebase Ltd and anor* [2002] 24 EG 134.
2   *Crestfort v Tesco Stores Ltd* [2005] EWHC 2480.

9.19 To return to the controls on the content of sub-leases, the landlord would wish additionally, that they:

- prohibit dealings in part;

- prohibit further sub-leases;

- give the head landlord proper qualified control of assignations; in this respect the clause should be framed so as to preserve clearly the rights of the head landlord[1];

- provide rent payment dates and a rent review pattern identical to the head lease;

- provide a right of physical entry for the head landlord.

These further controls are usually adjusted without undue difficulty.

---

1 *Sears Properties Netherlands BV v Coal Pension Properties Ltd* 2000 SCLR 1002, 2000 GWD 14–551.

9.20 The basic purpose behind the type of clause discussed in paragraphs 9.11–9.19 is that of controlling those who can acquire any security of tenure over the subjects of lease. In this respect the tenant's solicitor should realise that relatively informal or short agreements to occupy, designed as 'licences', may still include all the required elements of a lease and may be held to be such. In contrast to the more liberal regime in England[1], our courts will treat these documents as leases[2] for which the consent of the landlord would usually be required in terms of the type of alienation clauses under discussion albeit differentiating between a lease and a licence is not always without difficulty. The breadth of the normal drafting in such a clause serves to prohibit also all occupational rights but the landlord is usually content to accept from the tenant revisals to dilute control over some types of occupation, provided that, crucially, they are expressed so as to exclude any possibility of the occupant acquiring security. The usual provisions are:

- allowing a related company of the tenant into occupation in part or whole. The landlord would wish (a) details intimated and (b) occupation to cease when the occupier/tenant relationship ended.

- in retail property, allowing concessionaires or franchisees into occupation provided that (a) details are intimated (the tenant could argue that this is impractical), (b) there is a maximum area, and (c) the appearance of one trading unit is preserved as the landlord does not want a market style of operation to develop.

---

1 See eg *Bruton v London & Quadrant Housing Trust* [1988] QB 834, [1997] 4 AllER 970, [1997] 2 EGLR 91.
2 *Brador Properties v British Telecommunications plc* 1992 SLT 490.

Virtual Assignments

9.21 The febrile state of the property market a few years ago when many high value portfolio transactions took place contributed to the emergence of 'strange new beasts in the forest'[1] called virtual assignments. This was a concept designed by commercial property lawyers in the City of London intended to allow the timeous completion of a transaction despite concerns that the head landlords of some of the leasehold properties might refuse or delay the grant of consent and thereby prejudice or frustrate a vital deal. The arrangements also had other commercial benefits. The 'beasts' also crossed the border but not in great numbers.

---

1   *Clarence House Ltd v National Westminster Bank plc* [2009] EWCA Civ 1311 (at para 47).

9.22 The arrangement is somewhat complicated but has the effect of passing to the purchaser all of the economic benefits and burdens of the leases with an obligation to deal with the head landlord and all sub-tenants as though assignments (assignations) has been completed; all monies from the sub-tenants and any proceeds for renunciations belong to the purchaser. Conversely the purchaser indemnifies the seller for the tenant's financial and other obligations under the head lease. A power of attorney enables the purchaser to act as agent to the seller. The purchaser is not given any right of occupancy.

9.23 The issue that arises is whether such a device is effective in eliding the controls in the alienation provisions of a normal commercial lease, a matter that ultimately came before the Court of Appeal in England in the *Clarence House*[1] case. It had been held in the original case that the virtual assignment did not breach the prohibitions against assignation or subletting or granting a declaration of trust but did breach that against sharing possession or occupation. The Court of Appeal discussed at length the mechanism employed and concluded that the actings of the purchaser in its dealings with the landlord and sub-tenant were as an agent even although any money collected immediately became theirs. Accordingly the seller has not shared or parted with possession and the appeal succeeded.

---

1   *Clarence House Ltd v National Westminster Bank plc* [2009] EWCA Civ 1311.

9.24 There has been the predictable consequence of some landlords extending the alienation provisions to include the prohibition of virtual assignments. However there must be some question about the justification of that course of action, given that the landlord retains rights to sue its tenant for rents etc and to irritate the lease if thought appropriate. The argument deployed is that of justified concerns of the landlord that a tenant would divert sub-rents to a virtual assignee and thereby dilute its covenant. But landlords cannot control in any way what their tenants do with their income nor indeed how they generally conduct their affairs.

9.25 So far as Scotland is concerned the question of whether our courts would reach the same conclusion is perhaps unlikely to be addressed unless there are more sorties by these 'strange new beasts' into our territory, a possibility that seems unlikely at this time.

USER/KEEP-OPEN

9.26 User (or use) provisions in a lease (whether in one clause or several) will cover (a) matters upon which the landlord will require proper behaviour in the interests of other nearby properties and the public generally, (b) the nature of the business that can be conducted, and (c) whether the tenant is to be subject to an obligation of continuous trading (a 'keep-open' clause). These considerations apply in most leases but arise most acutely in a closed environment. Accordingly the relevant issues are most easily illustrated in a lease of a unit in a modern shopping centre.

9.27 The landlord should prohibit the tenant from any activity that could cause nuisance, damage or injury to the landlord or other tenants. Words like 'annoyance' or 'inconvenience' may be regarded by tenants as too general in scope for inclusion. Similarly, noxious or offensive trades or illegal or immoral acts are barred, although 'immoral' is often debated. Other behavioural requirements preventing accumulation of rubbish, avoiding damage to drains, preventing the placing of excessive weight on the structure, avoiding machinery likely to cause undue vibration and matters of that nature are prudent precautions for the landlord and no sensible tenant offers objection in principle. Of more difficulty are controls regarding the emission of noise if the tenant is, for example, in the audio-visual business or generally in industry. In that respect (and more generally) conditions in planning permissions must be observed strictly.

9.28 The specific user clause is often adjusted without undue difficulty, particularly when the heads of terms have incorporated the 'standard' user of the tenant. However, this should not blind advisers to certain underlying issues of importance, including the relationship of user to clauses on planning, rent review and alienation. Such issues will include:

9.29 If the specific user clause were fought out on the battleground of user alone, landlord and tenant would be at opposite corners. The objective of the landlord, most obvious in a shopping centre, is control, whether over tenant mix or (more difficult) over the quality of the retail offer. The landlord may have a contractual commitment to another tenant or tenants, limiting certain types of trade (para 2.37 and paras 10.7–10.10). These are very important financial considerations to the parties and the question of their susceptibility to attack on competition grounds is discussed in Chapter 10. In other types of property, the existence of a licence for a profitable use would militate against the landlord's willingness to grant consent for a different, less valuable, purpose. In contrast, the tenant's preference is for an unrestricted user, having in mind that the property needs to be capable (physically and in terms of the user clause) of use (a) for its initial intended purpose, (b) for any extension or variation of purpose (which may be necessary due to expansion of its operations, technological advances or changing market conditions over the period of the lease), or (c) ideally for the business, certainly if broadly similar, of an assignee. Lacking such freedom, the tenant would need consent when, possibly forced upon the tenant by changing market conditions, its needs changed; the landlord's control over alienation would extend beyond issues of covenant (para 9.4).

9.30 Ironically, an identical consideration, namely impact on rent review, forces both landlord and tenant out of their respective corners. As discussed in para 8.43, the hypothetical lease contains (unless stated otherwise) the terms of the actual lease. If, therefore, in comparison with the leases from which the rent review comparables are derived, the hypothetical lease contains a user clause which is either highly restrictive or unusually wide, the rent on review will be altered and one of the parties will suffer. Attempts by landlords to overcome this mutual problem from their perspective by the assumption for rent review of a wide user provision have generally failed (para 8.43) and the courts (in England) have resisted arguments that a rent review valuer can allow the possibility of a relaxation of the user clause[1] or that the landlord could widen it unilaterally[2].

---

1   *Plinth Property Investments Ltd v Mott, Hay and Anderson* [1978] 249 EG 167.
2   *C & A Pension Trustees Ltd v British Vita Investments Ltd* [1984] 272 EG 63.

9.31 Many user clauses refer to the prevailing Use Classes Order under planning legislation. Reliance on definitions which group together uses of a broadly similar nature provides clarity and brevity. Indeed the authorised planning use is the basis for the user clause, given the tenant's need to comply with planning legislation (para 9.50). Of course, any subsequent changes to or re-enactment of the Use Classes Order (the present one dating from 1997, albeit some indications emerged in 2010 that changes were under consideration) could result in a divergence between the lease definition and that for planning purposes but that would apply if the user clause had relied on its own definition. However, it would be unfortunate if a later order had the effect of changing a lease by, for example, modifying or even excluding a use class upon which the lease proceeded. Care should be taken to avoid a statute interpretation clause having that effect.

9.32 The parties need to adjust a clause that has no consequential impact on rent review and which, although not offering to either an ideal degree of control, will meet their respective needs. The following matters should be borne in mind:

- the style of clause that prohibits all uses except that specific to the tenant prevents the unintended omission of any undesirable uses;

- the specific use may be sufficiently wide to avoid any further drafting. For example 'a use within Class 2 of the Town and Country Planning (Use Classes) (Scotland) Order 1997' might satisfy both parties (although landlords often want to avoid office use including certain types of government offices). That said, it needs to be recognised that this use is confined to financial, professional or other services appropriate to a shopping area and where these services are provided principally to visiting members of the public. It does not extend to a use within Class 4, introduced to cater for so-called high technology uses which are environmentally acceptable in residential areas. Such distinctions in planning law give rise to difficulty and care should be taken in placing unguarded reliance on planning definitions;

- in contrast, a landlord of a shopping centre will rarely accede to a request for an open Class 1 user, having in mind concerns about trade mix and retailer profile. In consequence, the specific use is usually a description of the nature of the tenant's retail offer (sensibly, from the tenant's perspective, with some degree of flexibility). Having in mind the concerns of both parties as expressed in paragraph 9.29, this may be too limiting and the user may be extended to include any other (non-food) use within Class 1, subject to qualified consent (paras 9.3–9.10). In a shopping centre (as opposed to a retail park), the landlord's concerns about trade mix and the quality of retailing may result in a further qualification that consent may be withheld if in either of these matters the landlord thinks it prudent. The end result will depend on relative commercial strength, with a few major tenants able to demand a Class 1 user;

- occasionally, particularly where the use is unusual, parties may be tempted to define the use by reference to the business of the named tenant. This is not recommended, for a variety of reasons, not least because of a potential lack of clarity, whether it relates only to the business of the original tenant (definitions are relevant) or to the business of that tenant if it changes over time and worries by both parties on effects on rent review and alienation;

- when adjusting the user clause, the landlord's solicitor must prohibit all uses which conflict with contractual obligations already undertaken to other tenants (para 2.37).

9.33 The relevance to the user clause of the planning position has already been mentioned. Two specific areas should engage the attention of both parties:

- The tenant must ensure that the authorised planning use is consistent with the user clause, particularly where the lease contains a provision specifically avoiding any warranty by the landlord. A failure by the tenant in this respect is fatal[1]. Thus satisfied, the tenant knows that any change in the authorised use (however unlikely) demanded by the planning authority would be accompanied by compensation[2]. That authorised use may be contained in a planning consent (where the conditions would be highly relevant), one of the old-style certificates of established use or a certificate of lawful use or development; where the building is old and has been used for its purpose for many years (eg a shop in a high street), the tenant may have to accept the position without evidence.

- it is common, particularly in retail park developments, for the planning consent, or a related agreement under Section 75 of the Town and Country Planning (Scotland) Act 1997, as amended by the Planning etc (Scotland) Act 2006 to impose specific user restrictions by, for example, limiting (by number of units or their size) the sale of certain types of goods (eg electricals). Both parties need to be certain that the user clause does not offend such restrictions, having in mind the other outlets authorised in that manner, including those (if any) whose user clause is an Open Class 1 consent.

---

1   *Robert Purvis Plant Hire Ltd v Brewster* [2009] CSOH 28.
2   Town and Country Planning (Scotland) Act 1997, s 83 (as amended).

9.34 Closely connected to (and often part of) the user clause is the provision dealing with 'keep-open'. The landlord wants the tenant to be required (a) to take possession, use and occupy the subjects of lease within a stated period from the date of entry, and (b) to continue in physical occupation throughout the lease. Rarely would tenants wish to pay rent without occupying so that in practice discussions on (a) are often confined to the length of the period and the need to reflect the possibility of force majeure. That said, major tenants may resist where there is a long lead-in time before the property is to be ready, with an attendant risk of being obliged to fit out and trade from a unit that no longer fulfilled their needs. In contrast, (b) provokes intense controversy. The concern of the landlord is most easily understood in the context of a shopping centre where the departure of the anchor tenant to a rival development leaving a void will impact on the rents achieved on review, create uncertainty, provoke other departures and discourage investment in the centre. However, acceptance of the clause could leave a tenant obliged to trade from a loss-making property in a failing centre, losing market share to a nearby competitor in a new centre. In such a climate of depressed rental levels, escape by assignation may be impractical and an incautious approach to the constraints imposed by the landlord on sub-rents (para 9.16–9.17) may leave the tenant doubting the quality of the advice it received. Both parties have genuine concerns and in these circumstances the keep-open clause may be the 'deal-breaker', with the result being entirely dependent on commercial strength. If the landlord fails in its bid to include the clause, it will certainly want the tenant to maintain the external appearance of a trading unit (however unconvincingly) by the maintenance and illumination of an attractive window display. Of course, keep-open clauses are more difficult to justify in non-retail property or single properties where the landlord does not have a larger investment to protect. If the lease is to contain a keep-open clause there are some issues to consider:

9.35 Over many years tenants often accepted keep-open obligations in the belief (in which they found some support from *Grosvenor Developments (Scotland) plc v Argyll Stores Ltd*[1] and *Postel Properties Ltd v Miller and Santhouse plc*[2]) that the courts would not grant a decree of specific implement. That this might be an incautious approach began to be suspected in the late 1990s when, in a series of cases[3], views were expressed in favour of such orders, culminating in *Highland & Universal Ltd v Safeway Properties Ltd*[4]. There, the Inner House refused to be drawn into a comparative analysis of the position in Scotland and England because of a fundamentally different approach in that latter country. It was held that, save in circumstances of exceptional hardship or where such a remedy would be inconvenient and unjust, a party to a contract governed by Scots law, in contrast to its counterpart in England, is entitled to enforce such contractual obligations by a decree of specific implement. The lesson for the tenant is to assume that a keep-open clause will be enforced in its terms.

---

1   *Grosvenor Developments (Scotland) plc v Argyll Stores Ltd* 1987 SLT 738.
2   *Postel Properties Ltd v Miller and Santhouse plc* 1993 SLT 353.
3   *Church Commissioners for England v Abbey National plc* 1994 SLT 959; *Retail Parks Investments Ltd v Royal Bank of Scotland plc (No 2)* 1996 SLT 669; *Co-operative Insurance Society Ltd v Halfords Ltd (No 2)* 1998 SC 212, 1999 SLT 685.
4   *Highland & Universal Ltd v Safeway Properties Ltd* 2000 SLT 414.

9.36 The task for the landlord's solicitor is to provide specific drafting which avoids arguments about the clause being void from uncertainty. Given the approach of the court in *Highland & Universal Ltd v Safeway Properties Ltd*[1], words that require trading from the property as a whole during usual hours of business in the retail trade would appear to be sufficient. The core trading hours (and indeed the question of Sunday trading) are often identified clearly in modern leases where they have considerable application to service charge. A reference to such a definition would put the keep-open obligation beyond doubt in that respect. Of course these hours are also important if the intention is to restrict the tenant from operating outwith defined times. The tenant of a self-contained property would not wish to be so restrained. Office tenants may wish to operate outside normal business hours. Shop tenants may need servicing during the night. These practical matters and the implications on service charge should be capable of sensible resolution. An example of the tenant failing to persuade the court that the lease was too vague is found in *Oak Mall Greenock Ltd v McDonald's Restaurant Limited*[2].

---

1   *Highland & Universal Ltd v Safeway Properties Ltd* 2000 SLT 414.
2   *Oak Mall Greenock Ltd v McDonald's Restaurants Ltd* 2003 GWD 17–540.

9.37 The tenant's solicitor should qualify the clause to make proper allowance for closure during works of repair or refurbishment. Frequently, tenants also want the right to quit where they are engaged in bona fide efforts at alienation. Landlords may accept this but at worst must limit the period of closure and would do well to prevent closure until missives are in place with the new tenant to whom the landlord had consented.

9.38 A landlord may choose, depending on the prevailing circumstances, to seek damages for a breach of a keep open clause, rather than require specific implement. Such were the circumstances *of Douglas Shelf Seven Ltd v Co-operative Wholesale Society Ltd*[1] In the original case[2] the landlord of a lease in a Dundee shopping centre had succeeded in its claim and in the later action then sought an order requiring the tenant to carry out identified repair costs. It was held that, by electing to sue for damages, the landlord was not prevented from seeking specific implement of other obligations of the tenant under the lease.

1   *Douglas Shelf Seven Ltd v Co-operative Wholesale Society Ltd* [2009] CSOH 3.
2   Reported at [2007] CSOH 53.

ALTERATIONS/SIGNAGE/TRADE NOTICES

9.39 The tenant's need to consider, before commitment, the alterations which it requires to make at the outset has been discussed in paragraph 2.29, given the application of the clause or clauses in the lease which deal with alterations and signage. These three elements including trade notices usually appear in separate clauses but may conveniently be considered together. In respect of these matters the aim of the landlord is to preserve proper control, avoid paying compensation, retain the option at termination of requiring removal and reinstatement or of leaving the alterations and at rent review to rentalise improvements and disregard any diminishing effect. These issues are considered in turn:

9.40 The landlord's principal concern on control relates to structural and external changes. On structure, many landlords insist on absolute control and indeed have that control when the structure is reserved. Tenants may resist absolute control over external appearance where, for example, the tenant may plan a new shop front. Qualified consent (paras 9.3–9.10) might be thought appropriate, with some tenants demanding the right to carry out all alterations or signage without any consent if in their usual corporate livery and symbols. Landlords willing to concede this may want to consider a grant personal to that tenant. On office signage, a tenant taking for its corporate headquarters the whole block (or a major part) may wish to name the office accordingly; it is sensible for this to be negotiated as part of the heads of terms. Internal non-structural alterations are often allowed by landlords without consent, provided that they are notified to enable the consideration of any insurance implications. Experienced landlords and tenants know that in practice a tenant may often move partitions around and carry out minor works without the knowledge of the tenant's head office, let alone attend to the formal notification procedures in a lease. Trade notices create problems for the landlord in shopping centres. There must be sensible control over the nature, extent and positioning of such notices to enable the landlord to control the tone and appearance of the centre for the benefit of inter alia the other retailers. Some retailers would cover most of their window space if not constrained.

9.41 The absence of any common law right of the tenant to claim compensation for improvements is often fortified by a precise clause to that effect.

9.42 The landlord may include in the lease a clause requiring the tenant at termination to remove all alterations, signage etc and reinstate or, in the landlord's option, to leave them. The tenant may argue that such an option could prove very costly (paras 11.25–11.27) and could be a disincentive to future capital investment by the tenant to the advantage of neither party, such that the matter is best left for negotiation of the terms of the licence for works (or alterations) at which stage the details of the intended works are known. There is force in that argument but the landlord will wish to avoid discussions later about whether insistence on the option of reinstatement can be justified in terms of the qualified consent provision in the lease. A tenant who takes a lease with such an option of reinstatement should bear this in mind when negotiating the terms of a subsequent licence for works.

9.43 The rent review implications of major alterations are very important and are considered in some detail in paragraph 8.54.

9.44 The terms of any consent to be granted by the landlord are set forth in a licence for works which will bear some similarity to a fitting-out licence (para 2.29) and which will be prepared by the solicitor for the landlord. Apart from the obvious matters of recording the consent of the landlord to the proposed works identified by reference to plans and a specification, it will require the production of and compliance with all required statutory consents and with the Construction (Design and Management Regulations 1994), detail how and to what standard and within what timescale the works are to be completed, allow for site inspection and monitoring of works and require insurance information to be notified to the insurers and their approval obtained (para 2.29). There will be an indemnity to the landlord for any losses suffered and the tenant will be liable for all expenses. However, aside from these standard clauses that should be capable of ready adjustment, parties need to have particular regard to the works that are planned in the following two respects, having regard to the lease terms:

1. As discussed in paragraph 8.54, a disregard of any effect on rent of works for which the tenant has paid (whether this produces an adjustment that is upward or downward) is widely regarded as equitable. For a lease drawn on that basis, the licence for works should be silent on the point. However if the lease were, by its particular terminology, to disregard only 'improvements' which increased the rent, the landlord should try to alter this in the licence on the argument that otherwise it would be reasonable to withhold consent. Conversely, a tenant with a lease (that may have been inherited) containing review provisions that did not effectively disregard tenant's works that would enhance rental levels would be expected to negotiate appropriate changes to the review clause if contemplating major expenditure which would be to the general benefit of the landlord.

2. As mentioned in paragraph 9.42, the principle of reinstatement may or may not have been settled in the lease. In either event parties may want to look again at this in the knowledge of the alterations proposed.

9.45 However, in general, neither party with a lease in clear terms on rent review should allow a subsequent licence for works (or a fitting-out licence) to change the rental implications of alterations without a clear understanding of the consequences.

9.46 In respect of any planned alterations, the tenant may find itself obliged to apply for and obtain consent in terms of both the alterations clause and that dealing with planning (para 9.50). The tenant may wish to provide that consent given under one regime will be deemed to apply also to the other. The landlord needs to watch that it is still entitled to trigger the grant of a fitting-out licence or licence for works.

Green Issues

9.47 In respect of works by the tenant to the subjects of lease the following items may need consideration:

- In principle, and subject to the availability of all required consents, the tenant should try to obtain the right to install voltaic cells or panels or other sustainable energy equipment on the roof of the subjects of lease.

- The landlord will argue that, where practicable, whether in fitting-out (para 2.29) or when carrying out alterations, the tenant should use materials from sustainable sources.

- The landlord is likely to argue that any alterations which impact adversely on the environmental performance of the subjects of lease, or the larger development (including the EPC) should be within the landlord's absolute control and even if expressed to be subject to qualified consent, a refusal is reasonable if an adverse effect on carbon emissions would result.

- The tenant will wish to argue that there should be no requirement for removal of works (and consequent reinstatement) that contributed to energy efficiency

and, more generally, the tenant may be invited to accept obligations of the same nature that fall upon the landlord (para 10.11);

- To provide to the landlord information on energy and water consumption and to allow access for inspection.

- Not to do anything to adversely affect the EPC rating or the energy characteristics of the subjects of lease.

- To co-operate with the landlord in relation to any energy saving or carbon reduction initiative in relation to the whole development, provided that this does not breach any of the obligations of the tenant.

COMPLIANCE WITH TITLE AND STATUTE

9.48 In practice, such obligations may appear in various different locations but they share one common feature. They are all expressed as an obligation of compliance by the tenant, irrespective of the precise matter requiring attention. Consequently, their ambit may be sufficiently wide to encompass matters which are clearly intended elsewhere to fall outwith the responsibility of the tenant, for example the need to demolish a dangerous building following insured risk damage. For that reason, the tenant may wish to exclude any obligations relative to matters that fall within the obligation of the landlord under the lease.

9.49 The clause dealing with statute generally is often separated from that relating specifically to legislation on planning, and more recently, environmental matters. The matter that the tenant needs to understand is that the obligation extends beyond rectifying any breach of statute to require performance of any newly enacted requirement. A tenant could be compelled to reduce working space to produce a fire corridor and may, unless the tenant's solicitor has resisted the point, find itself disregarding these works for rent review purposes (para 8.54).

9.50 The need for the tenant to research the planning position prior to taking the lease is mentioned in paragraph 9.33. Thus satisfied, including on the matter of the authorised use and any conditions relative thereto, the tenant can in principle accept the requirements of the general planning clause aimed at the continuing need to comply.

9.51 It will address inter alia these points:

- no application should be made by the tenant without the landlord's qualified consent;

- the tenant should not be entitled to enter into an agreement under section 75 (para 9.33) without the landlord's qualified consent. Given that such an agreement should properly include the landlord (and all others in the leasehold chain including the head-landlord and secured creditors) some may argue, but in most cases to no avail, that this is unnecessary;

- implementing a permission should require the landlord's qualified consent. Given that implementation would negative the previous consent, this is sensible from the landlord's perspective;

- if the tenant, with authority, starts the authorised work, it must be finished, including the completion of all works detailed in conditions. The landlord does not want to be left at termination with work yet to be done, albeit it is likely that the landlord could require performance also under the licence for works.

9.52 The environmental legislation to which specific, as opposed to generic, reference began to appear in leases is that relating to the partial transposition into domestic law by virtue of the Energy Performance of Buildings (Scotland) Regulations 2008[1] of Article 4(3) of Directive 2002/91/EC of the European Parliament, requiring the production from 4 January 2009 of an energy performance certificate ('EPC') when a building is sold or leased. (See para 2.60).

---

1   No 309 as amended by 389.

9.53 On 1 April 2010 the CRC Energy Efficiency Scheme (the 'CRC') came into force[1]. This is a mandatory emissions trading scheme across the UK applying to large businesses (there are electricity consumption criteria) and public sector organisations requiring them to estimate annual energy usage and with effect from April 2011 to purchase allowances to cover CO_2 emissions. That purchase cost is then recycled to participants (the scheme is designed to be revenue neutral) by reference to a league table of participants judged generally on reductions of carbon emissions, a public record that may also have implications for the reputation of the bodies concerned and with possible market implications. These are the revenue recycle payments or RRPs, about which, in the context of the landlord/tenant relationship there has been much discussion. Responsibility for the CRC lies with the party contracting with the electricity supplier so that a tenant to whom the whole property is let will be responsible. In a multi-let situation the landlord may be responsible for some or all of the units and for the supply to the common parts. CRC participants need to aggregate consumption throughout the group. One has to decide who is responsible, who pays for the cost of the allowances and who gets the RRPs. With the passage of time the best solutions may present themselves and, although the introductory phase is intended to run until 2013, discussions on simplification are already taking place. At present the CRC is likely to be found in service charge provisions but, as discussed in paragraph 6.40 there are difficulties.

---

1   CRC Energy Efficiency Scheme Order 2010 (SI 2010 768).

DECORATION

9.54 The usual current painting cycle is three and five years for external and internal decoration respectively. Where the lease excludes structure there may be little, if any, external painting which falls within the tenant's responsibility. The landlord would wish to exercise qualified consent over the colours of external painting and of all decoration at termination.

Chapter 10

The Landlord's Obligations

INTRODUCTION

10.1 Unless otherwise provided in the lease, certain obligations fall upon the landlord at common law. Those relating to the condition of the subjects of lease at entry and its subsequent maintenance in tenantable repair are usually overcome in the lease (paras 5.4 and 5.5). That leaves the requirements to (i) give to the tenant at entry exclusive possession of the whole subjects of lease and (ii) maintain the tenant in such possession. These are discussed in paragraphs 10.2–10.4. The contractual obligations of the landlord may be found throughout the lease on such as provision of insurance cover (paras 7.4–7.6), reinstatement of insured risk damage (para 7.14) and services (para 6.10), although the underlying cost is commonly borne by the tenant. As a result of these various factors, any section of a lease entitled 'Landlord's Obligations' tends to be brief and in paragraphs 10.5–10.10 obligations that could be relevant to such a section are discussed. No matter the way in which the lease treats obligations of the landlord, the tenant's solicitor needs to ensure that all relevant schedules are triggered by a clause in the lease. Lastly, by way of introduction, obligations of the landlord granting a sub-lease are discussed in paragraph 12.11–12.13.

COMMON LAW OBLIGATIONS

10.2 Those that commonly survive specific contractual provisions to the contrary are:

10.3 that of providing possession of the whole of the subjects of lease, including all rights necessary for the tenant's proper enjoyment thereof. As discussed in Chapter 3, it is good practice to specify fully all such rights, common and otherwise, (paras 3.8–3.12) and from the landlord's perspective, to narrate all exceptions and reservations (paras 3.13–3.17).

163

10.4 that of maintaining the tenant in its possession. Paton and Cameron[1] state that '*The essence of this obligation is to be found in the absolute warrandice which will be implied in any lease in the absence of express stipulation to the contrary. The tenant's title is warranted at the date of entry, and the landlord is precluded from any action which may encroach upon the tenant's possession throughout the period of the lease. This limitation placed upon the landlord can also be stated in terms of the principle that a granter may not derogate from his own grant*'. Such was the principle laid down in *Huber v Ross*[2]. However, derogation requires some deliberate or voluntary act of the landlord; there is no implied obligation making a landlord liable for damage caused by third parties whom the landlord could not control or for whom the landlord was not responsible[3]. It follows from implied absolute warrandice that specific drafting is unnecessary. That said, the tenant's solicitor is not relieved of the need to carry out a proper examination of the landlord's title (para 2.3), not least because the landlord cannot be expected to disclose every burden and the tenant may be shown to have been put on notice. Nevertheless, those suffering from English influence often draw or revise leases to state that the tenant 'shall peaceably and quietly hold and enjoy the subjects of lease without any lawful interruption by the landlord or any person rightfully claiming through, under or in trust for it', or some such equivalent. Not only is such extravagant drafting unnecessary, it may mean less than the simple implied Scottish equivalent as the restriction to actions of the landlord etc would not seem to offer the tenant protection against eviction by an unconnected third party who successfully challenged the landlord's title. If one is impelled to state something on warrandice, words such as 'The Landlord warrants this lease absolutely' are sufficient.

---

1   Paton and Cameron *Landlord and Tenant* (p128).
2   *Huber v Ross* 1912 SC 898.
3   *Chevron Petroleum (UK) Ltd v Post Office* 1986 SC 291, 1987 SLT 588.

CONTRACTUAL OBLIGATIONS

10.5 Such obligations will be distributed throughout the lease, leaving any section of other contractual obligations to be limited to the type that follow:

Repairing Obligations

10.6 As mentioned in paragraph 10.1 the obligations of the landlord for repairs and reinstatement that arise either from (i) its insurance obligations (including where the landlord accepts responsibility for damage caused by a risk against which cover is unavailable) or (ii) service charge will be found in those discrete clauses in the lease. However, the tenant may have negotiated other limitations to its repairing obligations such as (a) a restriction to internal repairs (para 5.17), (b) by reference to a schedule of condition (para 5.18) or (c) by excluding latent defect (para 5.19). To avoid a gap in responsibility it is necessary, in respect of any of these matters which are relevant, to require the landlord to start any such work on receiving reasonable notice and to complete the same in a good and workmanlike manner within a reasonable period. In that respect the tenant may, in the event of failure by the landlord, contemplate doing the work and recovering the cost from the landlord. The same kind of disadvantages apply as if the roles were reversed (para 5.23) unless the tenant is minded to set off the cost against rent, a remedy that would leave the tenant in breach and its lease susceptible to irritancy if its common law right of retention had, as is usual, been contractually overcome[1].

---

1   *Skene v Cameron* 1942 SC 393.

Exclusivity Clauses

10.7 There is no common law principle that prevents a landlord from competing with the business of the tenant or allowing another tenant in its development to do so[1]. For that type of protection the tenant needs a contractual remedy. The question of retail trade rights exclusive to a tenant was considered in paragraph 2.37 in the context of the agreement or a back letter. Such exclusivity clauses are of considerable commercial importance and their inclusion in the lease, albeit that some landlords may be concerned to preserve commercial confidentiality, is important to the prospect of their survival on a sale of the landlord's interest. The apparent reservations expressed by Lord Macfadyen in *Optical Express (Gyle) Ltd v Marks and Spencer plc*[2] about whether such clauses were *inter naturalia* of a lease seem to have been resolved with the increasing importance and inclusion of such clauses in shopping centre leases. In that respect, Lord Drummond Young was able to conclude in *Warren James (Jewellers) Ltd v Overgate GP Ltd*[3] that the exclusivity clause was *inter naturalia* of such a lease and was accordingly binding upon singular successors of the landlord. In that case the drafting of the clause was roundly criticised but the court held that the landlord was in breach, a decision upheld on appeal[4]. The same parties re-engaged in that dispute in 2010[5] when the argument was whether the tenant's claim for damages in respect of a different breach of the same clause had prescribed. In this matter the landlord succeeded on the basis that the obligation to pay damages had prescribed for all purposes after 5 years, notwithstanding that some loss continued thereafter. The interpretation of such clauses can be dependent on their precise wording and, given their commercial significance, care is needed. In *Geoffrey (Tailor) Highland Crafts Ltd v Attractions Ltd*[6] attention centred on expert evidence on the meaning of 'accessories' in the context of 'Scottish highland dress and accessories'. It was held that the term did not extend to broadswords, claymores or tartan scarves and hats such that the landlord could retail these items. Interestingly, these same parties debated an implied trade restriction in 2010, resulting in the landlord being prevented from using for retail purposes an 'administrative office' so described in the lease with reference to a right of access reserved to the landlord[7].

---

1   *Craig v Miller* (1888) 15R 1005; *Geoffrey (Tailor) Highland Crafts Ltd v GL Attractions Ltd* 2010 GWD 8–142.
2   *Optical Express (Gyle) Ltd v Marks & Spencer plc* 2000 SLT 644.
3   *Warren James (Jewellers) Ltd v Overgate GP Ltd* (Unreported) [2005] CSOH 142.
4   *Warren James (Jewellers) Ltd v Overgate GP Ltd* (Unreported) [2007] CSIH 14.
5   *Warren James (Jewellers) Ltd v Overgate GP Ltd* [2010] CSOH 57.
6   *Geoffrey (Tailor) Highland Crafts Ltd v GL Attractions Ltd* 2002 GWD 24–776 (Sh Ct).
7   *Geoffrey (Tailor) Highland Crafts Ltd v GL Attractions Ltd* 2010 GWD 8–142.

10.8 Exclusivity (and also user) clauses now need consideration in the light of the Competition Act 1998 (Land Agreements Exclusion Revocation) Order 2010 which by revocation of a previous exclusion had the effect of applying from 6 April 2011 the force of competition law to 'land agreements', whether dated before or after that date. In the context of leases, this has impact on provisions which limit either (a) the commercial activity of a tenant for the benefit of the landlord or other tenants or (b) the freedom of the landlord to let other premises to competitors of the tenant for the latter's benefit. Any such provision, no matter the precise drafting, which has an appreciable effect on competition, is void and also has the capacity to taint other contract terms. An affected third party could take action in the courts to have such a restriction declared void and to claim damages and the Office of Fair Trading has powers to impose fines, albeit it is thought unlikely to be applied to land agreements.

10.9 In all cases to determine if competition is really affected requires a proper economic analysis in relation to the goods or services supplied within the relevant market area, the determination of that being crucial. An assessment of whether leases of a particular shopping centre containing provisions limiting the centre to one department store are truly restricting competition needs to consider the presence of any other department stores within a radius determined by a shopping impact analysis. The market place for a standard unit tenant, and whether and to what extent it went beyond the centre, would be somewhat different. Restrictions in leases affecting parties below certain market thresholds would be regarded as *de minimis*. There is also an important exception where it can be shown that the restriction brings economic and consumer benefits, is no more restrictive than is necessary to achieve such benefits and does not substantially eliminate competition. One can envisage a shopping centre developer intent on providing exclusivity to a department store or other anchor tenant arguing that the centre would bring substantial economic benefits, that an anchor tenant is needed to attract lettings and that no anchor tenant would sign up lacking the exclusivity protection.

10.10 During its transitional period the extension of the 1998 Act to property contracts provoked some concern within the property industry, particularly given the general nature of the guidance from the Office of Fair Trading[1] issued towards the end of that period. For example, the assessment of whether a party to a relevant agreement has the degree of 'market power' to which the guidance makes somewhat general reference in paragraph 1.9 will not be free from difficulty and it remains to be seen whether exclusivity clauses, which continue to be agreed, suffer serious attack.

---

1   Office of Fair Trading, *Guidance on Land Agreements*: March 2011.

Green Issues

10.11 The following obligations of the landlord could be considered appropriate for inclusion in a lease with green credentials:

- Where the subjects of lease are part of a development controlled by the landlord, the provision to the tenant of evidence, appropriately certified, that all building elements and systems within the development have been installed and are operated at maximum efficiency.

- Not to do or omit to do anything which affects adversely the EPC rating or the energy characteristics of the subjects of lease and to use, where practicable and in a proper manner, materials from sustainable sources.

- The provision to the tenant of information on energy and water consumption and on waste management in so far applying to the common parts of a development.

10.12 Obligations such as these may, at least in part, appear in service charge provisions in leases where the landlord controls a larger development and they also mirror some of the obligations that fall upon the tenant or tenants (para 9.47).

Chapter 11

Termination

11.1 The principal reasons which will trigger the termination of leases are:

- *rei interitus*/frustration;
- failure of a superior lease;
- irritancy;
- operation of a break option;
- agreement on early termination;
- proper notice, effective at the natural expiry date;
- rescission.

Many of these raise important procedural and financial issues and will be discussed in turn.

REI INTERITUS AND FRUSTRATION

11.2 Termination by operation of *rei interitus* is rare because the demands of the modern landlord for an uninterrupted rental stream result in most leases eliding the doctrine (paras 5.10 and 7.13), although often introducing new termination options linked to expected reinstatement periods following upon insured risk damage (para 7.14) or damage by an uninsured risk (para 7.10). A lease can nevertheless be terminated by a non-physical event, such as compulsory acquisition, which would frustrate the performance of the contract[1].

---

1   *Mackeson v Boyd* 1942 SC 56, 1942 SLT 106; see also *Robert Purvis Plant Hire Ltd v Brewster* [2009] CSOH 28.

FAILURE OF SUPERIOR LEASE

11.3 As discussed in paragraph 2.3, a sub-lease will fall on the irritancy of a superior lease and solicitors acting for a tenant in a sub-lease should alert their clients to the risk and if appropriate try to forge a direct contractual link with the proprietor of the dominium utile.

11.4 Such irritancy protection agreements can take a number of forms but the principal aim is to require a landlord, on its irritating a lease, to enter into a new lease with the sub-tenant for the unexpired residue on the same terms, including rent, as applied to the irritated lease. Not all superior landlords are amenable to this for a variety of commercial reasons and a complicated leasehold structure and/or the sub lease being of part only of the subjects in the superior lease make such an irritancy protection unlikely.

11.5 It should be recorded, firstly that statutory protection for a sub tenant exists on the termination of an interposed superior lease[1], secondly, a sub-lease does not fall by renunciation of a superior lease[2] nor thirdly, is it at risk of the extinguishment confusione of a superior lease[3].

---

1   Land Tenure Reform (Scotland) Act 1974, S.17
2   See Rankine *The Law of Leases in Scotland* (3rd edn, 1916 p193).
3   *Howgate Shopping Centre Ltd v Catercraft Services Ltd* 2004 SLT 231.

IRRITANCY

11.6 The so-called 'bare' irritancy clause used formerly (and occasionally currently) in our leases provided the landlord with an option to end a lease without compensation to the tenant if the latter failed to make a financial payment within a stated period (often 21 days) or was otherwise in breach or suffered a change in status, for example liquidation. The clause preserved the right of the landlord to all remedies for pre-termination breaches and the irritancy was declared to be incapable of being purged. Landlords also reserved another (but much less commonly used) means of attack, ie rescission, by deeming all such breaches to be material. The financial consequences, direct and indirect, of a forced vacation of a property from which a tenant was operating successfully might have very damaging, possibly fatal, consequences for the tenant. Furthermore, the lack of any compensation deprives the tenant of the value of its interest. It is true that occupational leases with a common rent review pattern (upon which this book focuses) often do not attract substantial values but those where the tenant has installed an expensive fit-out or other improvements (if not peculiar to the tenant's business) and/or where a sudden increase in general rental levels occurs in the early part of the review period may be very valuable indeed. And finally, the value of the tenant's interest in a ground or development lease can be very substantial. The dangers for the tenant seem obvious but despite the clarity of the terminology, the solicitors for many tenants accepted such clauses without demur, presumably on the basis that, like a legal irritancy, they could be purged or that somehow a court would inject some equity. Such illusions were shattered by the case of *Dorchester Studios (Glasgow) Ltd v Stone and anor*[1], where in the leading judgment, Lord Fraser of Tullybelton, said that 'it has been well established for at least 100 years now that a conventional irritancy in a lease for failure to pay the rent punctually is not purgeable unless it is being enforced oppressively'. Failure to warn the tenant did not constitute oppression[2]. As we shall discuss, the Dorchester Studios case[3] provoked two distinct responses, one immediate, the other less so.

1   *Dorchester Studios (Glasgow) Ltd v Stone and anor* 1975 SC (HL) 56, 1975 SLT 153, HL.
2   *Lucas's Exors v Demarco* 1968 SLT 89.
3   *Dorchester Studios (Glasgow) Ltd v Stone and anor* 1975 SLT 153.

11.7 The immediate response was the universal production by those solicitors acting for tenants previously unconcerned by bare irritancy clauses of protective clothes for their clients, many of whom were based in England and were shocked to learn of their apparent vulnerability. The precise terms of the qualifying clause which emerged after discussion between parties varied from case to case but the general objectives were to provide protection for:

- monetary breaches;
- non-monetary breaches;
- a secured lender;
- a change in status of the tenant.

These could be achieved in several ways. No breach capable of being remedied (albeit late) would found an action of irritancy unless and until the landlord had given written notice (preferably by recorded delivery and sent also to any registered office) under express threat of irritancy (to ensure that the tenant realised the potential consequences of inaction) requiring the breach to be remedied within a reasonable period stated in the notice and which in the case of a monetary breach would be a stated minimum period (the usual range was 14–28 days) and the tenant had failed to remedy timeously. Creditors in standard securities qualifying under the lease and intimated to the landlord (para 9.14) would be given notice and they, along with liquidators, trustees or receivers would be given a period (usual range 6–12 months) to assign, with the landlord being required to treat any application as though made by the tenant. Any landlord accepting this principle would require the third party within, say, 28 days of appointment to pay any financial arrears and sign a formal undertaking accepting personal liability (or providing a suitable guarantee) for the obligations of the tenant (except any keep-open clause) and that from the date of appointment until the entry of an authorised assignee. It should be appreciated that this contractual protection regime is generally capable of being agreed between parties, a matter which should have been taken into account in any consideration of future legislative change; where the type of lease concerned is a ground lease or premium lease or similar, the tenant's advisers may wish to extend the period of grace, possibly to require a second formal notice and even to dispense with the element of dealing with the status of the tenant.

11.8 The less immediate consequence of the *Dorchester Studios* case was statutory change found in the Law Reform (Miscellaneous Provisions) (Scotland) Act 1985, ss 4 to 7 and which followed from a report by the Scottish Law Commission[1]. Tenants, including those in leases which pre-dated the Act's operation (with a minor exception), were given these protections:

 • no financial breach would be the basis for an action of irritancy unless the landlord had given written notice to the tenant (sent by recorded delivery unless the landlord was unaware of any address for service in the United Kingdom) stating that the lease may be terminated if full payment is not made within the period specified (at least 14 days or, if longer, the unexpired balance of any days of grace for payment); [1]

- a landlord could not terminate on the basis of a nonmonetary breach or a change in circumstances of the tenant if in all the circumstances a fair and reasonable landlord would not so rely. The circumstances are stated to include whether the tenant has been given a reasonable opportunity to remedy the breach;

- these protections extended to attempts by the landlord to rely on these circumstances being (or being deemed to be) a material breach of contract.

---

1   Report on Irritancies in Leases (Scot Law Com no 75 (1983)).

11.9 In contrast to the form of contractual protection regime outlined in paragraph 11.7, the Law Reform (Miscellaneous Provisions) (Scotland) Act 1985 (a) did not require a notice for a monetary breach to spell out the consequences of continued failure, (b) ignored heritable creditors and (c) failed to distinguish between a non-monetary breach and a change in status of the tenant.

11.10 Although tenants welcomed the new protections of the Law Reform (Miscellaneous Provisions) (Scotland) Act 1985, the perception that they were too modest led most practitioners to continue with contractual protection in the lease and thereby to sideline the statutory regime. Over time, decisions by the court, such as the following, have vindicated that approach:

11.11 The limitations in the protection of the interest of a tenant with a valuable interest in a development lease were exposed in a long-running battle over Cumbernauld's main shopping centre[1]. In essence, Dollar Land had acquired for a substantial sum the interest of a tenant entitled to the centre's occupational rents, subject to a proportion of such rents being payable to its immediate landlord. Dollar Land had a history of erratic rent payments and its landlord served notice under the Law Reform

(Miscellaneous Provisions) (Scotland) Act 1985, s 4, threatening irritancy if payment was not made by a date exceeding the statutory minimum. On subsequent failure, the landlord declared an irritancy, required removal and rejected the late payment instantly offered by the tenant on realisation of its position. The case proceeded to the House of Lords where, unsurprisingly, the irritancy notice was upheld. In two subsequent efforts Dollar Land, taking solace from encouraging views of the court, argued for compensation for termination of a joint venture and then for unjustified enrichment. The tenant failed both in the Inner House and in the House of Lords[2] although judicial fears were expressed that valuable commercial development might be frightened away. It should be noted that the proposals of the Scottish Law Commission discussed in paragraph 11.13 indicated that such fears are groundless.

---

1   *CIN Properties Ltd v Dollar Land (Cumbernauld) Ltd* 1992 SC (HL) 104; 1995 SLT 669.
2   *Dollar Land (Cumbernauld) Ltd v CIN Properties Ltd* 1996 SLT 186; 1998 SC (HL) 90.

11.12 The phrase 'if in all the circumstances of the case a fair and reasonable landlord would not seek so to rely' contained in the Law Reform (Miscellaneous Provisions) (Scotland) Act 1985, s 5 was examined by the court in two cases where irritancy notices followed the appointment of a receiver to the tenant[1]. Both cases, in which the court found for the landlord and where it was held that the test was what a fair and reasonable landlord would have done, showed the difficulty of being required to come to a decision based on all the circumstances. In contrast to these two cases involving a change of status, the case of *Euro Properties Scotland Ltd v Alam and Mitchell*[2] brought s 5 into play in the context of a monetary breach. There the court did find for the tenant on the basis that a fair and reasonable landlord would not rely on the defender's failure to comply with a repairing obligation to irritate the lease but would instead carry out the repairs and recover the costs of doing so. However, in *Euro Properties* Lord Macfadyen stated *obiter* that post-irritancy events could be relevant to s.5 of the 1985 Act. In *Maris v Banchory Squash Racquets Club Ltd*[3] the basis for that view was held to be unsound, the proper date being that on which the action of declarator of irritancy was raised.

1   *Blythswood Investments (Scotland) Ltd v Clydesdale Electrical Stores Ltd* (in receivership) 1995 SLT 150; *Aubrey Investments Ltd v DSC (Realisations) Ltd* (in receivership) 1998 GWD 31–1623; 1999 SC 21.
2   *Euro Properties Scotland Ltd v Alam and Mitchell* 2000 GWD 23–896.
3   *Maris v Banchory Squash Rackets Club* [2007] CSIH 30; 2007 SC 501.

11.13 In October 2001, the Scottish Law Commission published further provisional proposals to reform the law of irritancy in commercial leases. In summary, the proposals for further legislative reform would, if enacted, be very similar to the contractual protection regime outlined in paragraph 11.7, save that the Law Commission seemed unconvinced about the need to provide statutory protection for third parties such as heritable creditors. In any event, nothing has been heard on these proposals since 2003, leaving practitioners to continue to agree conventional irritancy clauses of the type discussed in paragraph 11.7 or rely on the more limited protection afforded by the 1985 Act. Such contractual irritancy clauses will include the appointment of an administrator as an event of irritancy and would provide protection for the administrator in the same way as for such as a liquidator or receiver. Two possible concerns of landlords about administration orders have been addressed by the courts. The Insolvency Act 1986 at section 8 provides that during the subsistence of an administration order, 'no other proceedings and no exception or other legal process may be commenced or continued' against the company except with the consent of the company or the court. In the lease considered in *Scottish Exhibition Centre Ltd v Mirestop*[1] the appointment of an administrator was an event triggering irritancy. The court held that 'other legal process' did not include a non-judicial step and the appointment of the administrators ad interim allowed the pre irritancy notice to be sent. The question of whether a fair and reasonable landlord would enforce the irritancy was a matter for the court to determine on the facts. The second and related concern was the extent to which the landlord would be entitled to rent during the administration given that the intention of the administration procedure is to provide breathing space. This matter has received attention in the English courts, including in *Goldacre (Offices) Ltd v Nortel Networks UK Ltd (In*

Administration)[2] where it was held that the relevant Insolvency Rules were mandatory and that if rental liability fell within those rules then it was payable with the court having no discretion on the matter. That this is also the position in Scotland was clarified in a petition by Cheshire West and Chester Borough Council in the administration of Springfield Retail Limited[3]. The administrators of a Scottish company which was the tenant of a property located in England paid rent only until the date on which they stopped trading. Thereafter, the property was occupied by a third party to whom the administrators had sold the company's assets but no consent to that occupation was given by the landlord who ultimately changed the locks and thereby in English law terminated the lease. The occupants did not pay any rent which was then demanded by the landlord as an expense of administration. That claim succeeded. The Lord Ordinary was clear that this was not a legal process against the company, but a complaint against the administrators who had permitted what was described as a flagrant breach of the terms of the lease. There was no discretion in the application of the rules of the Act and rent was due as an expense of the administration. The court had no sympathy for the administrators, making it clear that had discretion played any part the result would not have differed. The message is that administrators in their negotiations for disposal of assets need not involve the landlord but nor can they disregard the interests of the latter.

---

1   *Scottish Exhibition Centre Ltd v Mirestop Ltd (in administration) (No 2)* 1996 SLT 8.
2   [2010] Ch 455.
3   [2010] CSOH 15.

11.14 Disputes about the validity of notices are common and this will be discussed in relation to break notices (para 11.16), a fertile source of dispute in this area. In each of three cases in recent years, a pre-irritancy notice was declared invalid due to failure to comply strictly with the requirements of section 4 of the 1985 Act because:

(a)   it was not clear about the actions required by the tenant to avoid irritancy; the alleged rent arrears were due to a previous landlord but the notice omitted any reference to either an intimation that payment was due to the first landlord or the basis for payment to the second[1];

(b) the notice (dealing with the lease of a house) required payment within fourteen days of the date of the notice as opposed to its service. Arguments that strict compliance was unnecessary failed[2]; and

(c) service was effected by Sheriff Officer, not 'sent by recorded delivery', the phrase in the Act. On appeal the Inner House concluded that this expression must relate to the Royal Mail recorded delivery service; further, the use of the words 'sent by' reinforced that view. Nor did industrial action at the material time provide an answer for the landlord as the court drew a distinction between, on the one hand, the need to send a notice complying with the Act and, on the other, its receipt. One could send by recorded delivery to comply with the Act and use other means such as sheriff officers to ensure receipt, explaining the possibility of late receipt of the principal notice[3].

---

1   *Ashford & Thistle Securities LLP v Kerr* 2007 SLT (Sh Ct) 60.
2   *Tawne Overseas Holdings Ltd v Firm of Newmiln Farm* [2008] CSOH 12.
3   *Kodak Processing Companies Ltd v Shoredale Ltd* [2009] CSIH 71.

11.15 The necessary consideration of the need to avoid the unfair and oppressive use of the remedy of irritancy should not persuade parties that all tenants are potential innocent victims of greedy landlords. Many tenants are very wayward in the performance of obligations which are both clear and fair and in many locations such as industrial estates, very active management is needed on behalf of landlords. Irritancy is itself a somewhat blunt remedy. A landlord, facing a tenant of good covenant who is in material breach of repairing obligations, would find a willing recipient of an irritancy notice in respect of an unwanted property but that remedy would leave the landlord suing the former tenant for pre-irritancy failures (provided that right had been expressly reserved as mentioned in para 11.6) and with an income stream interrupted for an unknown period. The landlord must be cautious in accepting any rent after starting irritancy procedures. Each case demands a consideration of the whole circumstances, including the collection mechanism and the payment history[1]. Sometimes justice requires that personal bar should operate but a landlord should not be punished if its actings were reasonable. This was the result in *MacDonald's Trustees v Cunningham*[2] where the landlord had accepted rent, not from the individual whose sequestration was the trigger for irritancy, but from a company associated with the tenant and with whom the landlord had been in negotiations (which aborted) for the latter to take over the lease.

---

1   *HMV Fields Properties Ltd v Bracken Self Selection Fabrics Ltd* 1991 SLT 31; see also *Wolanski & Co Trustees Ltd v First Quench Retailing Ltd* 2004 Hous LR110.

2   *MacDonald's Trustees v Cunningham* 1997 SCLR 986 see also *Seahive Investments Ltd v Oisbanjo* [2008] EWCA Civ 1282.

OPERATION OF BREAK OPTION

11.16 Break options are usually, but not universally, tenant-only options, often coinciding with a rent review date. They are commercially important and those involved in adjusting the terms of the option and in the procedure for its later exercise need to exercise care throughout. The following matters need attention and have application to notices generally, not just those in relation to break options:

11.17 Clarity in drafting is needed on the operational mechanics of the break clause, including the date for service of the notice, the terms, address and mode of service, the precise identity of the parties (which may well have changed over time) and the effective date. Such details may be contained in the break clause itself or in a general clause in the lease (para 2.47) or both.

11.18 It is now settled law that, in disputes on the validity of a notice, there are two discrete points to be determined, namely, (a) whether the notice complies with the formal requirements of the break clause and, if so, (b) did it effectively convey the required information[1]. Such were the matters considered in two recent cases. In the AWD Chase case[2] the formalities of the break notice were held to be complied with and the debate then focussed on whether a reasonable landlord in the position of landlord in the lease in question would have understood the break notice to have been sent on behalf of the tenant when it had identified a different group company as such. On the facts of the case including the state of knowledge of the landlord, the Lord Ordinary upheld the notice. In doing so and in acknowledging the potential for confusion where a party to the lease was incorrectly identified, he referred to the need for a detailed analysis of the facts in each case and refused to place too much weight on decisions where the facts were not too dissimilar, particularly as these were English cases. In the second case[3] the difficulty for the tenant was a break notice addressed, not to the landlord but to an associated company. That was a failure to comply with the formal requirements of the lease and there was no need to consider the so-called 'reasonable recipient' test. That said, the break notice was upheld as, on further arguments, it was shown to have been served on an agent of the landlord with authority to receive the notice. The tenant was not so fortunate in *Prudential Assurance Company Ltd v Exel UK Ltd*[4] where the notice omitted the name of one of the two companies that constituted the tenant and the court considered that 'real doubt' would be generated about whether the notice was served also on behalf of the omitted company.

1 *Mannai Investment Co Ltd v Eagle Star Life Assurance Co Ltd* [1997] AC 749 (see paras 776A–C); *Scrabster Harbour Trust v Mowlem plc* 2006 SC 469 (see para 45); *Ben Cleuch Estates v Scottish Enterprise* 2008 SC 252 (see para 64).
2 *AWD Chase De Vere Wealth Management Ltd v Melville Street Properties Ltd* [2009] CSOH 150, 2010 SCLR 521.
3 *Batt Cables plc v Spencer Business Parks Ltd* [2010] CSOH 81.
4 [2009] EWHC 1350 (Ch). See also *Hotgroup plc v Royal Bank of Scotland plc* [2010] EWHC 1241 (Ch).

11.19 That these are times when many tenants are concerned to find relief from onerous leases and landlords sensibly scrutinise all break notices and act in such a way as to preserve such leases is shown by two recent cases in England. In the first[1] the landlord, aware of the tenant's intention to break the lease, delayed until after the break date the acknowledgement of the notice that was required for the purposes of the lease (that requirement following from other failures of the tenant) and thereby successfully resisted the break. In the second[2] the value to the tenant of a break notice was shown by a somewhat ambitious attempt to persuade the court that a right to break, expressed in the lease to be personal to the named original tenant, could be exercised after assignation; the attempt failed. One could also conclude that a significant proportion of the disputes is caused in part by companies and those acting for them displaying a casual approach to identification of group companies.

---

1   *Orchard (Developments) Holdings plc v Reuters Ltd* [2009] EWCA Civ 6.
2   *Norwich Union Life & Pensions (otherwise Aviva Life & Pensions Ltd) v Linpac Mouldings Ltd* [2010] EWCA Civ 395.

11.20 The following matters are also worthy of mention:

- In relation to compliance with the formal requirements of the break notice, the words 'not less than nine months notice' were held to exclude the first and last day[1], a notice for which proof of sending existed must be presumed to have been received lacking evidence to rebut that presumption[2] and ample evidence of the difficulties caused by inherently faulty drafting is provided by *Richmond Securities Ltd v Weatherhead (UK) Ltd*[3].

- The nature of a break clause and a reference to the need for a tenant to serve notice within a stated period are thought sufficient to make time of the essence but some leases specifically so state.

- A right to break is unilateral and its exercise brings the lease to an end. In *Allied Dunbar Assurance plc v Superglass Sections Ltd (No 1)*[4] the landlord failed in an argument that a tenant, in material breach, could not found on its exercise of a break option. However, some break options are expressed in the lease to be conditional on the tenant not being in breach of any obligation, monetary or otherwise. There is force in the argument that a negotiated break option is a fundamental condition for the tenant's taking of the lease and should be unfettered, given also the other remedies are available to the landlord. Nevertheless some tenants do accept that it cannot be exercised if the tenant is in material breach of a financial obligation. To go further and impose conditionality in respect of past and current breaches (even when remedied and no matter how trivial) may be thought unreasonable. A minor repair yet required to fully satisfy a schedule of dilapidations served close to the option date could be used by the landlord to frustrate the right to break. In *Trygort (No 2) Ltd v Home Finance Ltd*[5] the court decided that a historic breach remedied before the option was exercised would not deprive the tenant of its rights to terminate, preferring to opt for the commercially sensible construction. One can reasonably conclude that to achieve such an extreme purpose would require clear drafting.

- One should bear in mind that the existence of a break option will have valuation implications for rent reviews (para 8.42) and may operate as a contra-indication to the principle that time is not of the essence in such reviews (para 8.14)

- The only additional point to arise from the proper exercise of an option to break is the triggering of the landlord's right to serve upon the tenant a terminal schedule of dilapidations discussed in paragraphs 11.22–11.27.

1   *Esson Properties Ltd v Dresser UK Ltd* 1997 SLT 949, 1996 SCLR 1041 (OH).
2   *Chaplin v Caledonian Land Properties Ltd* 1997 SLT 384 (OH).
3   1998 GWD 1–46.
4   2003 SLT 1420.
5   2009 SC 100.

AGREEMENT ON EARLY TERMINATION

11.21 If parties agree to advance the contractual termination date, a renunciation will have the effect of terminating the lease. As is discussed in paragraphs 11.25–11.27, important considerations of dilapidations and reinstatement apply on termination. Where parties have agreed to advance that termination date, it is important that both are clear about these issues and that the missives for renunciation ideally annex a draft renunciation to put liability beyond doubt.

NATURAL EXPIRY

11.22 The certainty of the contractual termination date allows parties to plan ahead. A tenant considering major capital expenditure on the property during the last few years of the lease should first agree an appropriate extension of time such as would justify the expenditure. Similarly, a tenant content to extend should for practical and negotiating reasons allow time to organise alternative accommodation if talks fail. It is not prudent for a tenant to be negotiating an extension in the weeks leading up to the termination date, a consideration that applies equally to a landlord anxious to avoid an empty property.

11.23 However, leases do not automatically terminate despite phrases in the lease such as 'without any warning away or process of removal to that effect'. The requirements of notices are derived from the Sheriff Courts (Scotland) Act 1907, although few would claim that our law is crystal clear. Where the lease does not provide for a longer period, the usual period of notice for commercial leases is 40 clear days[1]. Parties must comply with any notice provisions in the lease[2] (para 2.47) setting aside any formal requirements notices require to be in a form clearly showing an intention to terminate and remove and parties would be sensible to adhere to the forms set out in the Sheriff Courts (Scotland) Act 1907. The 'reasonable recipient' test is discussed in paragraph 11.18. If a tenant, in receipt of a proper notice to quit, refuses to vacate, its actual physical removal is regulated by the Sheriff Courts (Scotland) Act 1907; conversely, if a tenant vacates a property, hands back the keys and cancels rental payment arrangements, a landlord who has failed to serve a proper notice but who wants vacant possession can safely assume that the lease is at an end.

1   *Signet Group plc v C&J Clark Retail Properties Ltd* 1996 SC 444.
2   *Esson Properties Ltd v Dresser UK Ltd*; *Capital Land Holdings Ltd v Secretary of State for the Environment* 1996 SC 109, 1996 SLT 1379, 1995 GWD 39–2030.

11.24 Tenants of commercial properties in Scotland have, unlike those in England, no statutory right of lease renewal. But tenants of shops have the limited protection afforded by the Tenancy of Shops (Scotland) Acts 1949 and 1964. Somewhat illogically, the protection is limited to head tenants[1].

The definition of a 'shop' is borrowed from the Shops Act 1950 and involves 'any premises where any retail trade or business is carried on'. It seems that the specific examples in the Shops Act 1950 would qualify but that the courts would be slow to admit into the definition premises where there is not a significant retail element as opposed to a sale of services[2]. A tenant of a 'shop' in receipt of a notice to quit can apply within 21 days to the sheriff court (failing which all rights are lost) for a renewal on such terms and with a duration not exceeding one year as the sheriff considers reasonable, no doubt bearing in mind the existing terms. The Shops Act 1950 gives examples where the sheriff would be entitled to refuse the application, for example where the tenant is in material breach or insolvent, where the landlord has offered suitable alternative property or where greater hardship would be caused by renewing than by allowing the lease to lapse. Inability to pay rent does not qualify as hardship[3]; this must be judged on the facts of each case but major tenants are not denied qualification simply because of their financial resources. Any renewal is deemed to be a new lease[4] and the tenant is entitled to further renewals, at least in theory.

---

1 *Ashley Wallpaper Co v Morrisons Associated Companies* 1953 SLT (Sh Ct) 25.
2 See *King v Cross Fisher Properties Ltd* 1956 SLT (St Ct) 79; *Oakes v Knowles* 1966 SLT (St Ct) 33; *Boyd v A Bell & Sons Ltd* 1969 SLT 156.
3 *Stenhouse v East Kilbride Development Corpn* 1962 SLT (Sh Ct).
4 *McMahon v Associated Rentals Ltd* 1987 SLT (Sh Ct) 94.

11.25 The natural expiry of the lease triggers important financial considerations for the parties in the shape of potential reinstatement obligations and relative to dilapidations.

11.26 Alterations and improvements, for which the tenant has no right to compensation, were considered in paragraph 9.42. At termination, therefore, the landlord should consider whether and to what extent the tenant should be required to reinstate and ensure that any notice is served properly in terms of the lease or the relevant licence for works. The tenant may realise, too late, that the original price of obtaining consent from the landlord, namely the latter's option of requiring reinstatement or the leaving of improvements, was very high.

11.27 Interim schedules of dilapidation and the remedies of the landlord during the subsistence of the lease were considered in paragraph 5.21. Those remedies at termination have narrowed to those of either doing the work and recovering the cost from the tenant or, more commonly, suing for damages. The basis for assessing loss causes difficulty. In England a combination of a common law rule (as affirmed in *Joyner v Weeks*[1]) and the Landlord and Tenant Act 1927, s 18(1) has the effect of measuring damages at the cost of doing the work capped at the diminution in value of the landlord's interest at the expiry date. In a recent English case[2] a landlord, unsure at the termination date (for reasons judged to be reasonable) whether to replace completely the defective cladding on a building but who subsequently did so, succeeded in its claim for the notional cost of repair of the cladding on the basis that the replacement work would not have been necessary had the cladding been repaired by the tenant in accordance with its obligations in the lease. The apparent flexibility of the decision has caused some concern but the Scottish courts have always tended to take a flexible approach. *Joyner v Weeks*[3] has never been part of our law[4] nor does the Landlord and Tenant Act 1927 have application here[5]. Our courts would be inclined to quantify the claim by reference to the cost of the work and consider averments that the true loss is materially less. Damages would be assessed as for any other breach of contract, including an assumption that the landlord had taken all reasonable steps to minimise its loss. In practice, most claims for dilapidations are ultimately settled between parties by a lump sum payment which is recognised by HM Customs and Excise as being outwith the scope of value added tax.

---

1 *Joyner v Weeks* [1891] 2 QB 31.
2 *PGF II SA v Royal & Sun Alliance Insurance plc* [2010] EWHC 1459/TCC.
3 *Joyner v Weeks* [1891] 2 QB 31.
4 *Duke of Portland v Wood's Trustees* 1926 SC 640, 1926 SLT 417.
5 *Prudential Assurance Co Ltd v James Grant & Co (West) Ltd* 1982 SLT 423.

Tacit Relocation

11.28 The failure by either landlord or tenant to serve proper notice as discussed in paragraph 11.23 results in the automatic continuation of the lease by tacit relocation on the same terms as the original lease, except for duration which will be for one year or for the length, if shorter, of the original lease. The extended lease can itself continue if no later notice is given. However, provisions in the lease incompatible with a renewal for one year (or shorter) do not apply, so that a tenant's option to renew was held to have been lost[1]. It may be possible to avoid tacit relocation in commercial properties by express exclusion within the lease[2].

1   *Commercial Union Assurance Co Ltd and Others* 1964 SLT 62.
2   *MacDougall v Guidi* 1992 SCLR 167.

RESCISSION

11.29 The right of either landlord or tenant to rescind a lease on the grounds of a material breach of contract does not seem to have engaged much attention but well drawn irritancy provisions have always preserved such a remedy for the landlord by declaring breaches by the tenant to be material (para 11.6). Also, as stated in paragraph 11.8, the protections afforded by the 1985 Act extended to attempts by landlords to rely on such a declaration. A few cases in recent years may signal some interest in the remedy of rescission. In *Central Car Auctions v House of Sher (UK) Ltd*[1] a tenant attempted to rescind a lease based on an alleged material breach of contract, this being a lease granted by its landlord of part of the roof of the subjects of lease for the installation of telecommunications equipment. It was held that the breach was not sufficiently material to justify rescission. In *Crieff Highland Gathering Ltd v Kinross Council*[2] the landlord, in the absence of an irritancy clause, tried to rescind on the basis of the failure of the tenant to comply with its repairing obligations. The court allowed the matter to go to proof as the maintenance obligation was at the heart of the contract, the rent being nominal. A possible issue that might be argued by a tenant as material to the contract could be the refusal of consent by a landlord, if judged unreasonable. Whether this would justify rescission is not certain but *obiter* remarks of the Inner House in *Scotmore Developments v Anderton*[3] offer encouragement in that direction (9.8).

1   [2006] CSOH 137.
2   *Crieff Highland Gathering Ltd v Perth & Kinross Council* 2010 GWD 22–431.
3   *Scotmore Developments v Anderton* 1996 SC 368, 1996 SLT 1304.

Chapter 12

Sub-Leases, Assignations and Renunciations

SUB-LEASES

12.1 Ideally, the tenant of an occupational lease will (para 9.15) try to negotiate the right in principle to:

- sub-let the whole of the subjects of lease, with the prospect of a profit rental until the next review and the flexibility of offering to the occupier a lower rent or diluted obligations in weak market conditions;

- sub-let parts of the subjects, either taken initially to accommodate future space needs or shown later to be surplus to current requirements.

12.2 The consent of the landlord will be required in relation to:

- the identity of the proposed tenant (para 9.14) in respect of which a financial information package will be required. The production by the tenant of piecemeal information is unhelpful to the landlord and may result in delay;

- the detailed terms of the proposed sub-lease (para 9.15); the landlord and its advisers will pay particular attention to clauses that could impact adversely on rental evidence and will review very carefully any dilution of obligations on the sub-tenant;

- any change of use proposed by the sub-tenant (para 9.28); a retail tenant may want to incorporate in the sub-lease a specific prohibition against a use competitive with its own but not so as to trigger a discount on rent of review;

- sub-division works if part only of the subjects of lease is involved (para 9.40); the landlord would find difficulty in resisting in

187

principle an application for such consent where the lease allowed partial sub-leases;

- the fitting-out works proposed by the sub-tenant (para 9.40) if made a condition of the missives;

- the grant by the landlord of the form of direct undertaking to the sub-tenant considered in paragraph 2.3 (v); the landlord should resist, particularly where part only of the subjects of lease is involved or the proposed sub-tenant is less financially secure than the tenant.

12.3 Although the landlord's solicitor should examine the proposed sub-lease, it is preferable to preserve the lease hierarchy by avoiding the grant of the landlord's consent *in gremio* of the sub-lease. A separate letter of consent will fix the duration of the sub-lease, require general consistency with the lease, prohibit prior entry, state the rent, confirm the rent review pattern, try to disregard the sub-rent as rental evidence in the lease, specify user, include any further alienation restrictions, preserve dilapidations claims against the tenant and impose a time limit for the payment of all financial arrears and the execution of the sub-lease. The landlord will expect the tenant to pay its administrative costs and the fees incurred to its solicitors and surveyors for the work involved and may ask for an early undertaking for these in case the matter aborts. Finally, any heritable creditor of the landlord needs to grant consent (para 2.3 (iii)).

12.4 It has already been acknowledged that, subject to any changes required by the parties and to which the landlord (and any secured creditor) has consented, the sub-lease requires to be consistent with the lease. Indeed, although weak market conditions may create difficulties for the tenant, its objective is to ensure that its responsibilities to the landlord are matched by its rights against the sub-tenant. Beyond these matters, the solicitor for the tenant has freedom in the manner of drafting the sub-lease and should take the opportunity to correct or improve drafting where the need for change is clear, for example intervening case law. But more extensive redrafting, albeit with the best of intentions, carries the risk of a mistake or omission which defeats the stated objective and a style different from the lease may be unwelcome to the landlord's solicitors. Whether the sub-lease should repeat *ad longum* the conditions of the lease (subject to the necessary changes) or incorporate by reference major sections of that lease (eg a schedule of tenant's obligations) is a matter of personal preference, provided that, by whatever method, the draft reflects the agreed heads of terms, the conditions of the landlord's consent and the consequential changes that flow from the grant of a sub-lease, particularly where part only of the original subjects of lease is involved. Among these matters are the following:

12.5 A sub-lease of part of the original subjects will need a clear definition of the property leased and any areas (eg an amenity block, common entrance or fire escape corridor) common to the property sub-let and the retained subjects. The responsibility for maintenance of any such common area and the sharing of the resultant cost needs treatment. Any new rights and reservations required as between the two properties need to be drafted. These are matters separate from any service charge payable by the tenant, an agreed proportion whereof needs to be refunded by the sub-tenant within a time scale that is consistent with the tenant's own obligations.

12.6 Attention has been drawn to the concerns of the landlord that the sub-lease should not produce unwelcome rental evidence, leading to a requirement that rent payment and rent review dates in the sub-lease repeat those in the lease (paras 9.15–9.19). To repeat the rent review clause is generally considered unwise and unnecessary. In normal circumstances (but see para 12.7) the tenant's objective is to equalise the rents after review and avoid net liability. The aim of the landlord is to obtain the open market rent unaffected by the existence of the sub-lease. Independent rent review procedures (despite identical criteria) are administratively inconvenient and admit the possibility of different rents. In essence, the tenant wants its sub-tenant to pay the rent agreed or determined on review between landlord and tenant, and some sub-leases so provide. However, to inject influence into the determination of the rent for which it will indirectly become liable, the sub-tenant should prohibit agreement without its consent, thereby leading to the comparative safety of third party determination in which the tenant would be compelled to advance the sub-tenant's representations. This concession is likely to be bought at the price of liability for all of the expenses of the procedure if the rent was not reduced from that originally proposed. Rent review clauses in sub-leases are more complicated where part only of the property is being sub-let. The necessary works of sub-division may have a depressing effect on the sub-rent so that the tenant faces a higher rent per square foot for the retained property than is being achieved for the sub-let property, all other matters being equal. Quantum discount arguments are also relevant. In these circumstances the parties may agree that the 'head rent' be apportioned according to floor area.

12.7 Occasionally, due to unusual circumstances, the objective of a tenant in an occupational lease when subletting is not to equalise the rent on the next review date but to obtain a profit rental. Such was the aim of the tenant in The *Howgate Shopping Centre Ltd v Catercraft Services Ltd*[1] who because of its previous ownership of some of the land on which a shopping centre had been built had negotiated a lease at a rent equal to 23% of the open market rent. A sublease was granted at an open market rent (so that the aim of a profit rent was met) but the review provisions were imported from the superior lease, leading to the sub-tenant arguing that the rent on review was 23% of the open market rent, thus depriving the head tenant of its profit (although the upward-only principle in a depressed market would slow that process). The court held that this was not a case where any help in construction could be gained from identifying the commercial purpose and that the objective conclusion was that parties did not intend the sub-tenant to benefit from the discount. Whatever the precise circumstances, the lesson is that a highly uncertain outcome can follow from ambiguous drafting.

---

1   2004 SLT 231.

12.8 It is open to the tenant to impose upon the sub-tenant a higher rate of penalty interest or a shorter period of grace for financial payments; indeed the latter may be a necessity to avoid cash flow penalties.

12.9 There may be specific additional controls that the tenant should impose such as on alienation or user. The sub-tenant will wish to bear in mind that, even if these controls would normally be regarded as unduly onerous with a potential for reducing rental levels, the form of rent review clause discussed at paragraph 12.6 would give no comfort to the sub-tenant.

12.10 Almost inevitably, and as considered in Chapter 7, the landlord will be insuring and recouping premiums from the tenant. The sub-lease should provide for payment to the tenant of the premiums for which the tenant has liability to its landlord; if from the date of entry to the next planned review date there is to be a profit rental, the tenant should consider the need for additional loss of rent insurance, given that abatement provisions will operate.

12.11 The tenant's solicitor should include in the sub-lease clauses that, in relation to access rights and the need for consent, include the landlord.

12.12 The sub-lease needs to set forth the obligations of the tenant *qua* landlord. These should include the payment of the head rent and more generally all obligations under the lease not passed on to the tenant (para 12.13) with indemnification provisions. The tenant should be under an obligation to use all reasonable endeavours to enforce the obligations of its landlord under the lease and, where the tenant is willing to grant consent (or requires to do so), to use reasonable endeavours to obtain the landlord's consent.

12.13 Although the sub-tenant may argue (para 12.12) that the tenant must comply with all of the obligations in the lease (unless specifically passed on) the tenant will wish the sub-tenant equally to do so except to the extent of being expressly stated to be the tenant's obligation. These 'catch-all' clauses are uncomfortable for parties and are avoided only by a very detailed sub-lease which militates against incorporation into the sub-lease by reference of general tracts of the lease, as considered in paragraph 12.4.

ASSIGNATIONS

12.14 The implied right of the tenant to assign having been excluded (para 4.3), the bases upon which the tenant may assign are considered at length in paragraphs 9.11–9.20. Although the procedure for acquiring or selling a leasehold interest by assignation is outwith the scope of this book, the following practical matters are worthy of mention:

12.15 A tenant, contemplating assigning its lease, has to apply to the landlord for consent to assign to the identified potential tenant and to any required change of use; if the proposals are sufficiently well advanced, the application may include fitting-out proposals. The application should be accompanied by a full financial package to reduce the prospect of delay (para 12.2). The alienation clause in the lease regulates the rights of the parties in relation to the application.

12.16 Assignation is a substitution in the identity of the tenant. A landlord consenting to an assignation is renouncing all claims against the former tenant except rent for the period ending with the assignee's entry, unless a joint and several obligation exists (paras 4.3 and 4.14). The assignee, whose title is incomplete until proper intimation to the landlord, becomes liable for the rent, probably including any arrears for the period prior to its entry. The solicitors for the various parties should bear these and other points in mind in relation to the documentation. The landlord's solicitor, in issuing any letter of consent, should try to ensure that:

- payment of all financial arrears, including interest, is made by the outgoing tenant prior to the agreed date of entry;

- although arguably unnecessary, the assignee undertakes to pay all financial payments from the date of entry and perform all of the tenant's other obligations referable to the period prior to or after entry;

- if a rent review has just been agreed, the rent review memorandum is fully executed prior to entry. The question of whether the landlord could legitimately withhold consent pending agreement on the new rent is more difficult (para 9.5) and may depend on the length of the delay;

- there is annexed to the letter a draft of the assignation to which the landlord (in contrast to a sub-lease) will be a party, incorporating by way of variation to the lease any change of use or other alteration required by the assignee concerned at any particular condition in the lease and to which the landlord is prepared to agree. The relatively common practice of the assignation imposing on the assignee obligations which precede the date of entry in order to guard against failure by the assignor is often resisted by incoming tenants on the basis that this is a negation of the common law position, and that the landlord is in the best position to know whether and to what extent the assignor is in breach and has obvious remedies, including the practical point of making relevant demands before consenting;

- the assignation will not bind the landlord nor will the assignee take entry until intimation evidenced by production of a certified copy assignation and a letter of obligation from the assignor's solicitors regarding delivery of extracts (usually two in number);

- the consent dies if intimation is not effected within a stated timescale;

- all the professional expenses are reimbursed.

12.17 If the tenant's solicitor is to accept a letter of consent in these terms (and most landlords would want a contract to that effect), he/she must ensure that any missives for the assignation mirror the relevant terms.

12.18 The proposed assignee needs to take the usual measures on title, local searches, the existence of conditions attached to or need for planning permission and also, should the obligations extend to the period before entry, obtain information on any that are outstanding. In particular the tenant needs to know that all alterations or additions have received landlord's consent and which of these are rentalised particularly where of recent vintage and not reflected in the current rent.

12.19 The assignation should be consistent with the terms of the letter of consent but otherwise will reflect the commercial terms agreed between the tenant and the assignee. The landlord is likely to resist a clause requiring acknowledgment that the tenant's obligations are fulfilled and no grounds for irritancy exist; to accept would require a full management inspection and survey.

12.20 The assignation will disclose any price being paid by either party to the other and that raises the subject of VAT. If the assignee is paying a price, this is exempt subject to the assignor's option to tax. The question of whether a payment by the assignor to the assignee attracts VAT was examined in *Commissioners of Customs and Excise v Cantor Fitzgerald International*[1] where the European Court decided that an agreement to accept the lease was a supply of services. The Sixth Directive, art 13 (B) (b) exempts leasing but not transactions based on leases and the supply by the assignee is taxable at the standard rate.

---

1   *Commissioners of Customs and Excise v Cantor Fitzgerald International* [2001] ECR I-7527, [2001] STC 1453, ECJ.

12.21 The assignation needs to be intimated to the landlord and the missives should identify which party should have that obligation and the timescale for doing so.

RENUNCIATIONS

12.22 When parties agree that a lease should be terminated earlier than its natural expiry date the matters which will engage the attention of the solicitors, aside from the usual conveyancing procedures, are in most cases limited to the following:

12.23 Just as with assignations, care must be taken in ascertaining the VAT position where an inducement is involved. In *Lubbock Fine & Co v Commissioners of Customs and Excise*[1], on a direct reference by a VAT tribunal, the European Court debated whether Customs were correct in charging VAT on a substantial payment from landlord to tenant. The Court decided that the Sixth Directive, art 13 (B)(b) exempting 'the leasing of immovable property' exempted also a change in the contractual relationship such as termination. As a result of this decision and subsequent legislative changes, a payment by the landlord to the tenant is exempt, subject to the tenant's option to tax, and a payment by the tenant to the landlord is exempt, subject to the landlord's option to tax.

---

1   *Lubbock Fine & Co v Commissioners of Customs and Excise* [1993] ECR I-6665; [1994] 2 CMLR 633.

12.24 On the agreed entry date, the liability of the tenant (and any guarantor) for the monetary obligations under the lease terminates. The landlord would expect the renunciation specifically to reserve all claims for such payments, notwithstanding its execution by the landlord; in practice, the landlord's solicitor should deliver the renunciation in exchange for all sums due.

12.25 The obligations of the tenant relative to reinstatement and dilapidations were considered in paragraphs 11.26 and 11.27 and in law the position is no different in relation to an early expiry by renunciation. In practice, however, particularly where the landlord wishes to recover possession (and may be paying the tenant an inducement) for major alterations or even total redevelopment, the tenant may expect to avoid all liability. The solicitors for the parties should obtain instructions on this point and narrate the agreed position in the renunciation following on missives to that effect.

Index